Back-to-School

MAILBOX® Magazine

Kindergarten–Grade 1

Great back-to-school ideas, activities, and reproducibles from the 1998 to 2002 issues of *The Mailbox®* magazine!

- **Getting Acquainted**
- **Organizational Tips**
- **Open House**
- **Birthday Celebrations**

- **Classroom Displays**
- **Parent Communication**
- **Classroom Management**
- **Art Activities**

And much, much more!

Managing Editor: Allison Ward

Editorial Team: Becky S. Andrews, Kimberley Bruck, Karen P. Shelton, Diane Badden, Thad H. McLaurin, Sharon Murphy, Karen A. Brudnak, Sarah Hamblet, Hope Rodgers, Dorothy C. McKinney

Production Team: Lisa K. Pitts, Pam Crane, Rebecca Saunders, Jennifer Tipton Cappoen, Chris Curry, Sarah Foreman, Theresa Lewis Goode, Ivy L. Koonce, Clint Moore, Greg D. Rieves, Barry Slate, Donna K. Teal, Tazmen Carlisle, Amy Kirtley-Hill, Kristy Parton, Debbie Shoffner, Cathy Edwards Simrell, Lynette Dickerson, Mark Rainey, Gina Farago

www.themailbox.com

Table of Contents

©2005 The Mailbox®
All rights reserved.
ISBN10# 1-56234-637-7 • ISBN13 #978-156234-637-9

Manufactured in the United States
10 9 8 7 6 5 4 3

Make a Splash!

Catch this big wave of back-to-school fun! Opening the school year with an ocean theme is a great way to get youngsters into the swim of things.

- Make waves across your classroom ceiling using blue crepe paper or fabric strips. Start by creating strips longer than the length of the room. Attach the ends of a strip to the ceiling at opposite ends of the room. Then attach the material to the ceiling at intervals to create a wavelike effect. Repeat the process, spacing the strips about three feet apart.

- Cover the classroom windows with pieces of blue cellophane. Simply trim the cellophane to fit each window and tape it to the window's edges.

- Embellish your walls with a variety of fish cut from fluorescent poster board. Use fluorescent paints to create designs on the fish. Then attach them at various heights on the walls. They'll seem to glow in the blue light. As an added touch, attach cutouts of green poster board seaweed for the fish to hide in and swim around.

Cast a Net

Use a welcome letter as your net to gather your little fishies together for the first day of school. About a week before school starts, send each of your new students a letter on ocean-themed stationery. In the letter, introduce yourself, tell about exciting activities that the child will get to experience, and let the child know how to find you on the first day (see "Here I Am!" on this page). If possible, put a photograph in the letter to help the child start to put your face with your name. Finally, include in the letter a tagboard cutout of a fish. Instruct each child and her family to decorate the fish any way they wish. Remind them to include the child's name somewhere on the front of the fish. Encourage the child to bring her fish to school on the first day to help you decorate the classroom. What a catch!

Donna Battista
Parkview Elementary, Valparaiso, IN

Here I Am!

Be easy to spot on the first day of school! Use some of the props listed below to help your new students instantly recognize you. In your welcome letter (see "Cast a Net" on this page), tell youngsters what to look for. Then don your gear on the first day and watch for big smiles!

Possible props:

sunglasses	wet suit	sun hat	beach towel (wear around
mask and snorkel	inner tube or swim ring	captain's hat	your neck or over your
flippers	boogie board	sailor suit	shoulders)
beach-print clothing	sandals or flip-flops	beach bag	sand shoes
			sand pail or shovel

adapted from an idea by Sylvie Audet-Faddis
Arthur Robinson P.S., Sudbury, Ontario, Canada

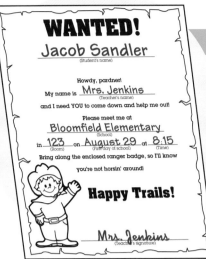

WANTED!

Jacob Sandler
(Student's name)

Howdy, pardner!

My name is Mrs. Jenkins
(Teacher's name)

and I need YOU to come down and help me out!

Please meet me at

Bloomfield Elementary
(School)

in 123 on August 29 at 8:15
(Room) (First day of school) (Time)

Bring along the enclosed ranger badge, so I'll know

you're not horsin' around!

Happy Trails!

Mrs. Jenkins
(Teacher's signature)

Write 'em, Cowboy!

One week before school begins, rustle up some excitement about the first day by sending your youngsters a letter! To prepare, make a copy of the letter on page 14. Program the letter with your name, the school's name, the room number, and the day and time that school begins. Sign the letter, make a copy for each child, and then program each one with a different child's name. Next, make a yellow construction paper star badge for each child. Personalize each badge and then laminate it. Mail each child his letter and badge. On the first day of school, dress in your best cowpoke attire. Greet each youngster with a hearty "Howdy!" and then pin his badge to his clothing. (Be sure to have extra badges for unexpected arrivals.) Yee-haw! What a way to start the year!

Hats Off to You!

Turn some heads on the first day of school with these personalized cowboy hats! To make one hat, duplicate the large cowboy hat pattern (page 15) onto brown construction paper. Laminate the hat and cut it out; then use a craft knife to create slits where indicated. Next, slide a 1½" x 24" strip of laminated paper through the slits as shown. Use a permanent marker to write the child's name on the strip; then staple the strips to fit the child's head. Howdy, pardner!

Line Up!

Use this idea to line up your little cowpokes with ease! To prepare, cut a pair of construction paper cowboy boot shapes for each child in your class. Label each pair with a number. Laminate the boots; then tape the pairs in numerical order near your door. Direct your line leader to stand on the first pair of boots, the second child to stand on the second pair of boots, etc. When your little ones are lined up, have them recite the rhyme below and then giddyup and go!

When buckaroos line up with folks,
There are no pushes, shoves, or pokes.
Their hands are still and by their sides,
Feet ready for a quiet ride.
Giddyup!

Materials Swap

Here's a fun way to recycle classroom materials that otherwise might be forgotten in a storage closet. During one of the teacher workdays at the end of the year, host a Swipe and Swap. Have each teacher bring from her classroom something that she's grown tired of or that she has an excess of. Place all of the materials on a table and give each teacher a number as she enters the room.

Now it's time to swipe and swap! The first teacher chooses an item from the table. The second teacher can swipe the first teacher's choice or choose an item from the table. The third teacher can swipe either the first or second teacher's choice or choose an item from the table. The game continues in this manner until everyone has had a turn. (To hurry the game along, you may want to limit the number of times an item can be swiped.) Then, at the end of the game, the first teacher to choose gets an opportunity to either keep what she has or swap with someone. This is a hilarious way to bring faculty together at the end of the year and find new homes for unused materials.

Linda Blassingame
JUST 4 Developmental Laboratory
Mobile, AL

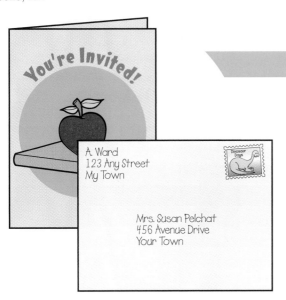

Reaching Out

If you're a brand-new teacher or new to your grade level, consider hosting an idea shower! Send shower invitations to teachers who teach in your district and at your grade level. Invite them to your home for dinner or party refreshments, and ask that each guest bring a successful classroom management tip, a favorite teaching idea, or anything a new teacher such as yourself could benefit from. Your hospitality and your eagerness to learn from your colleagues are sure to be well received!

Susan G. Pelchat—Gr. 2
Forbes School
Torrington, CT

Great Finds at Great Prices

Spend a few summer Saturday mornings rummaging through garage sales, thrift stores, or your local flea market. These places are gold mines for inexpensive books, toys, dramatic-play props, and other items that will enhance your classroom teaching. For practically pennies, you can start the year with some new-to-you instructional aids. One person's junk is truly a child's treasure!

Linda Blassingame

Into the Sharing Pool

Schools often buy one large set of manipulatives or other teaching aids and ask that the teachers on each grade level share. If this is your situation, try this method of organization. At the beginning of the year, put all of the shared materials in one place. Then divide the materials into as many groups as you have teachers. Label each group with a different letter. For example, the frog counters and Geoboards might be in group A, while the dinosaur counters and alphabet tiles might be in group B. Make a master list of which items are in which group; then have the teachers collaborate on a rotation schedule. You might decide to rotate the materials every month or every quarter. Then send each teacher off with her first group of materials for the new school year.

If you're lucky enough to have your own sets of materials, consider starting this type of sharing pool. Have the teachers on your grade level bring some different types of materials to put into the pool. Then divide the materials as described above and start sharing! It's a great way to gain access to a wider variety of instructional aids without having to buy them all. And now's a good time to organize the sharing pool so that the system is ready to go once school starts.

Ada Goren
Winston-Salem, NC

Pins for Pennies

Here's a quick and inexpensive way to create appealing pins for student wear. To make a class set of back-to-school pins, adhere on poster board one back-to-school sticker for each student. Then laminate the poster board or cover it with clear Con-Tact covering. Cut out the stickers and use craft or hot glue to attach a pin fastener to the back of each one. The unique welcome-to-school jewelry will make quite a fashion statement! Plan to create additional sticker pins to recognize student achievements, stimulate interest in topics of study, and celebrate student birthdays.

Ann Marie Stephens—Gr. 1
George C. Round Elementary School
Manassas, VA

Photo Craze

Next year's students and parents will look forward to the new school year after thumbing through this memorable album. As you collect photos this year, set aside a few each month that depict typical classroom events. At the end of the year, arrange all the photos in an album. During your visitations of incoming students, place the album beneath a sign that reads "Take a Look at This Book!" Encourage children and parents to get a feel for what they can expect in the coming year by looking through this special album.

Marlene Baker—Gr. K
Mars Hill Bible School
Florence, AL

All About You!

You've all had those precious little ones that respond with shock when they learn that teachers actually leave the school building in the evenings and do ordinary things, such as shop in grocery stores, walk their dogs, or eat at restaurants. Create an all-about-you book to help your new batch of students get to know you and feel more comfortable in your classroom. In advance, gather a collection of photos that show you in settings or situations that children are likely to find interesting, such as with your family, friends, pets, or on a vacation. Arrange and mount the photos on sheets of construction paper. Then add simple captions for each picture. Laminate the pages; then bind them together behind a laminated cover. Display this book during meet-the-teacher times and the first few days of school. This book will be in high demand!

Angela Van Beveren
Alvin, TX

This is my dog, Pepper.

Camping with my daughter.

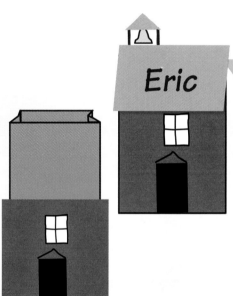

Eric

"Bag" to School!

Help ease your little ones' first-day jitters by welcoming each child to school with his own schoolhouse bag. To begin, glue on red construction paper to cover about two-thirds of the front of a paper lunch bag as shown. Next, fold down the top of the bag and glue on a construction paper roof and bell. Use markers and additional construction paper pieces to add details to the schoolhouse. Then use a paint pen to label the roof with a student's name. Place a few school-related items inside the bag, such as an eraser, a pencil, and a bookmark. Position each bag in a child's chair or on his table space. What a wonderful schoolhouse welcome!

Dawn Schollenberger—Gr. K
Mary S. Shoemaker School
Woodstown, NJ

Hugs and Kisses

No matter how old you are, making it through the first day of school deserves a hug and a kiss! In advance, purchase a supply of Hershey's Hugs and Kisses candies. For each child, wrap a Hug candy and a Kiss candy together in a square of tissue paper; then tie the tissue paper closed with a length of curling ribbon. At the end of the first day, tell your youngsters that they each deserve a hug and a kiss, and then hand them out!

Sandra Rice—Gr. K
Trinity Lutheran School
West Seneca, NY

A Special Space

Foster a sense of classroom ownership and belonging by inviting each child to create his own special space in your classroom. A couple of weeks before school starts, mail each child a notecard inviting him (and his parent) to drop by your classroom on a designated date. (Use your open house date if your school holds one before classes start.) In the note, ask the child to bring requested school supplies with him on that day. When the child arrives, show him his cubby and where any larger supplies of his will be kept. Then give him a strip of tagboard labeled with his name. Encourage him to use an assortment of simple art supplies, such as stickers and stamps, to decorate his nametag. Then help him post his nametag on his cubby or at a table space. Youngsters will rest easy knowing they have a special space in their new classroom. And you'll rest easy knowing all those sets of school supplies are organized before that hectic first day of school!

adapted from an idea by
Kiva English—Gr. K
Cato-Meridian Central School
Elbridge, NY

Oh, You'll Know!

Every parent who has dealt with the question, "How will I know who my teacher is?" will be forever grateful to you for this idea! Choose a symbol from a classroom theme or a book that you plan to read on the first day. Then design something with that symbol that you can wear. For example, if you plan to read *The Cat in the Hat,* make a red-and-white striped hat from a paper plate and construction paper. (See additional suggestions below.) A couple of weeks before school starts, jot a quick note to each child telling her that you will be the teacher wearing the tall, red-and-white striped hat. They'll know just what to look for!

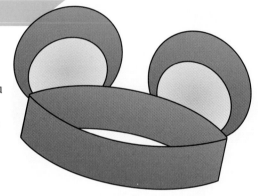

- For a teddy bear theme, wear a headband with teddy bear ears.
- For a T-shirt theme, wear a very colorful, oversize T-shirt.

Deb Scala—Gr. K
Mt. Tabor Elementary School
Mt. Tabor, NJ

A "Bear-y" Good Welcome

Comfort your new students on the first days of school with a familiar storybook friend, Corduroy! Introduce your stuffed pal to the group and then read Don Freeman's famous tale. Invite each child to hold Corduroy while you snap his first-day-of-school photo. Then take youngsters on a tour of the school as you try to find Corduroy's button. Other first-day activities can relate to buttons, such as sorting, counting, and patterning. (Because buttons pose a potential choking hazard, make a large supply of plastic milk caps resemble buttons by drawing buttonholes on them with a permanent marker.) Once Corduroy's button is found and sewed on, put him in a backpack along with a journal to make home visits.

Terri Strong, Santa Paula, CA

Follow the Flowers

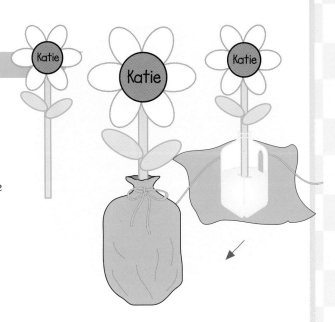

Your budding students will confidently follow these flowers right to your door on the first day of school. In advance, collect a class supply of milk jugs and wooden dowels. Paint the dowels green. For each child, cut out a large construction paper flower and leaves. Label each flower with a different child's name; then laminate all the flowers and leaves. Tape the flower and leaves to the stem. Then weight an empty milk jug with sand. Insert the flower stem in the sand. Next, loosely wrap tissue paper around the outside of the jug; then gather it at the top with twine. On the first day of school, arrange the flowers so that they make a path leading to your classroom entrance. Parents and children alike will bloom with delight over this personalized welcome to school.

adapted from an idea by Debbie Musser
Washington Lee Elementary
Bristol, VA

The Magic Apples of My Eye

Let each child know how important she is to you with a magic idea that plants a seed of wonder. In advance, cut out a large tagboard apple for each child in your class. Using a craft blade, cut out a square from the center of each apple. (Judge the size of the apple and the cutout square by the size of your Polaroid pictures—described later.) If desired, add a stem and leaf to each apple. Then mount a large tree cutout on a classroom wall. On the first day of school, take each child's picture with a Polaroid camera. Invite each child to hold her picture by the edges and watch as the "magic" happens! When each photo has developed, glue it to the back of an apple and write the child's name on the front of the apple. Mount each apple on the tree and title the display "The Apples of [Your Name]'s Eye!" After explaining the meaning of the title to your students, watch them shine with pride!

Lou Monger—Gr. K
Glen Allen Elementary
Glen Allen, VA

Nifty Nametags

Stick with this idea and you'll receive rave reviews from substitute teachers, guest speakers, and field trip chaperones. Use a computer to label several class sets of adhesive nametags. Keep a set or two in your substitute folder and then store the rest in a handy location for easy distribution. You'll save time and minimize confusion for everyone who is involved!

Sandy Preston
North Street Elementary
Brockway, PA

Colorful Nametags

Brighten up your class with these easy-to-make nametags. For each student, round one end of a 6" x 18" colored construction paper rectangle to resemble a crayon tip. Use a black marker to personalize and decorate the nametag. Then laminate the tag for durability and tape it to the student's desktop. What a vivid way to deck out desks!

Gina Parisi—Grs. 1–6 Basic Skills
Brookdale School
Bloomfield, NJ

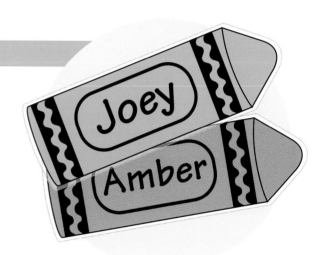

Student Information Cards

Send your new students' self-esteem soaring when you greet each child by name on the first day of school! To prepare, personalize an index card for each child and glue on his card a photocopy of the most recent school picture he has on file. On the back of his card, list his date of birth, a home and/or work number where a parent can be reached, known allergies, and so on. Hole-punch the cards and secure them on a loose-leaf ring. Then use the cards to learn the names and faces of your new group of youngsters. During the school year, leave the cards for substitute teachers, carry them on field trips, and share them with classroom volunteers. You'll find that these cards continue to be an invaluable resource long after the first day is over.

Landria Williamson
Copperfield Elementary
Taylor, TX

New Student Plan

Prepare for new student arrivals with a handy checklist! To make a checklist of things to remember for new students, list the information by categories. Possible categories include notes to send home, staff to notify, and items, such as desk nametags, to personalize. When a new student arrives later in the year, use a copy of the checklist to help ensure that no details are overlooked. A smooth transition is bound to be the result!

Lu Brunnemer—Gr. 1
Eagle Creek Elementary
Indianapolis, IN

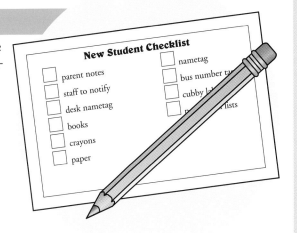

New-Student Welcome File

Make new-student arrival easy on yourself and the new child with this handy file! First, label an accordion file "Welcome, New Students!" Then label each of the inner compartments with a different supply that is needed throughout the school year (such as nametags, cubby labels, permission slips, monthly calendars, book-order procedures, etc.). File each supply in its corresponding compartment. When a new student arrives, simply pull one item from each compartment. In no time at all, you and your new student will be up and running!

Karen Griffin—Gr. K
Rainwater Elementary
Carrollton, TX

Mingling Manager

On that first day of school, do you have every intention of meeting and greeting each new child and parent with warmth and security only to be barraged by too many things happening at once? Here's a suggestion to ease that dilemma. Before students arrive, set up several play dough stations on your tables. If desired, offer written suggestions at each station to get the dough rolling, so to speak! When children and parents arrive, ask them to choose a place to work with the play dough. Because each parent and child is involved in this activity, you'll be able to meet and mingle at your leisure. You're also likely to find that this environment is a great one for students and parents to get to know each other as well. So let's get that dough rolling!

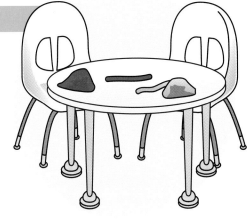

Leslye Davidson—Gr. K
Alameda, CA

No More Jitters

Ease your youngsters' first-day anxieties with a cuddly class mascot! Introduce a stuffed animal to your class and pretend that he is whispering in your ear. Reassure him that school is a fun, safe place to be and that the children are friendly and kind. Explain to students that your friend is feeling shy and nervous about starting a new school year. After students offer encouraging words and discuss their own concerns and fears, have your mascot guide them through each step of the day. It won't be long before your little ones feel relaxed and confident about school!

Jill Myers—Gr. K
Colstrip, MT

First-Day Fun

There's nothing like a little science to keep your mind off first-day jitters! To prepare, fill two containers with water. Tint one with blue food coloring and the other with yellow. Make enough tinted ice cubes so that each child will have one of each color. Give each youngster two ice cubes sealed in a zippered plastic bag. Ask her to melt the ice as quickly as possible; then watch the creative solutions in action! Have her observe her bag periodically. Hey, blue ice and yellow ice make green water!

adapted from an idea by Jeanette Pauls—Gr. K
Calistoga Elementary
Calistoga, CA

Are We There Yet?

"Is it lunchtime yet?" "When can we go outside?" "Is it time to go home?" Sure, all of these are very important questions to a child—but they also take up a lot of your time, don't they? This idea will help children understand the pace of each day as well as reinforce meaning and print. In advance, laminate a long strip of butcher paper. Glue a school cutout to the left side and a house cutout to the right side. Then use wipe-off markers to program significant times of your day along that strip. Next, add words, simple drawings, and/or pictures to depict your schedule for the first day of school. As you go through the first day, use reusable adhesive to post a cutout (such as a bus or other theme-related item) along the timeline. At the end of the day, program the timeline for the next day. As children become accustomed to this process, ask a child to move the cutout as the day progresses. I can read just where we are!

Angela Lavy Joel—Gr. K
Marlowe Elementary
Falling Waters, WV

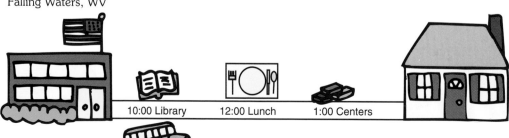

10:00 Library   12:00 Lunch   1:00 Centers

Toothy Tote Bag

Make the event of losing a tooth even more special with a toothy tote bag! Pack a canvas bag (or other carrier) with two or more tooth-related books, a small photo album, and a tooth-shaped writing journal. When a student loses a tooth, take a candid Polaroid picture of him for the photo album. Then seal the child's tooth inside an envelope and send it home in the tote bag. A child shares the contents of the bag with his family members and then, with their help, writes and dates an entry in the journal. Ask the child to return the tote bag—minus his tooth, of course—the following school day.

Kay Young—Gr. 1
Mt. Vernon Elementary
Clermont, GA

Tooth Taxi

To guarantee that a lost tooth arrives home from school safely, provide a Tooth Taxi for its transportation. Cut out a small picture of a tooth and label it "Tooth Taxi." Secure the picture to an empty film container with clear packaging tape. When a student loses a tooth, simply drop the tooth into the container and snap on the cap. The tooth will travel in style!

Dee Kaltenbach Riesen—Gr. 1
Tri County Elementary School
DeWitt, NE

Lost Tooth Certificates

Be prepared to share in the excitement when a child loses a tooth! Before school starts, purchase a supply of small resealable bags from a craft store. Then use your computer to design a page of colorful certificates, making sure the certificates fit inside the size of bag you purchased. Print several copies of the page and cut out the individual certificates. Keep the certificates and bags handy. When a student loses a tooth, write his name and the date on a certificate. Then seal the certificate and his tooth inside a bag for a safe journey home.

Deborah Bellinger—Gr. 1
White Oak Primary
White Oak, TX

WANTED!

_____
(Student's name)

Howdy, pardner!

My name is _____
(Teacher's name)

and I need YOU to come down and help me out!

Please meet me at

_____
(School)

in _____ on _____ at _____:_____ .
(Room)   (First day of school)   (Time)

Bring along the enclosed ranger badge, so I'll know

you're not horsin' around!

Happy Trails!

_____
(Teacher's signature)

Note to the teacher: Use the letter with "Write 'em, Cowboy!" on page 4.

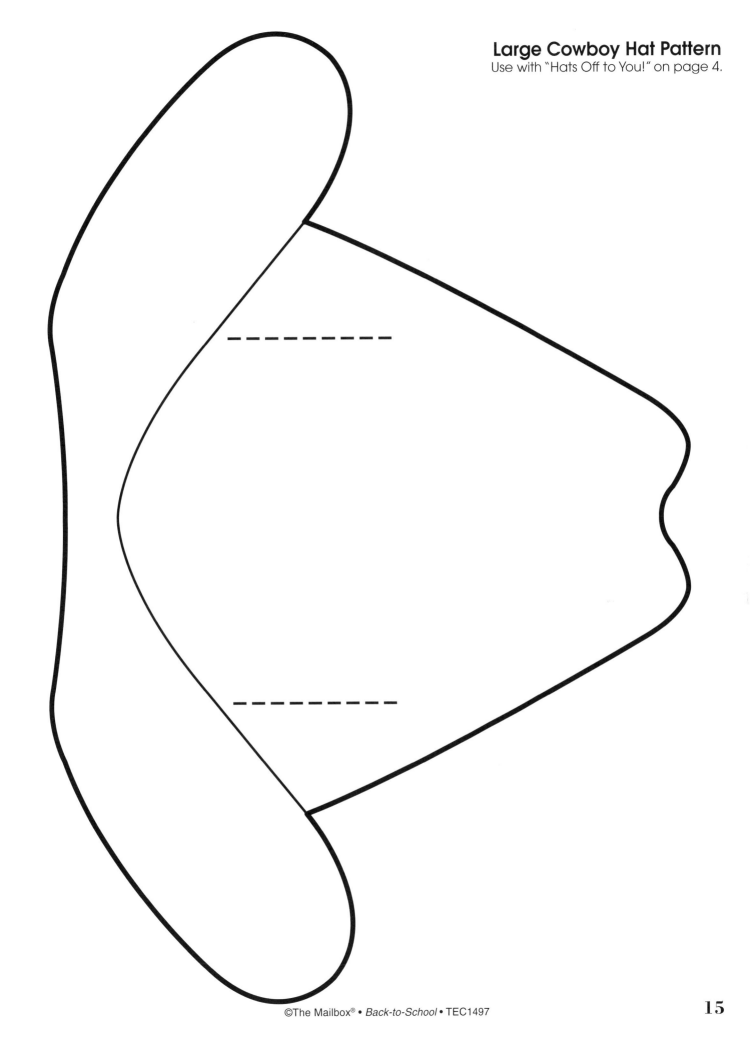

Apple Decor

When students set their eyes on this "a-peel-ing" door decoration, you'll hear a chorus of oohs and aahs! Cover the door and an area of wall space around it with white paper. Mount a red apple-shaped border around the door, trim away unwanted white paper, and attach a paper leaf and stem. Personalize a seed cutout for each child. Mount the cutouts on the door and then use chalk or crayons to add apple core details. Wow! What an awesome apple!

Joyce R. Welford
Sandra Smith—Teacher Assistant
Leakesville Elementary School
Leakesville, MS

Dive Into School

This inviting door decor will welcome your new students and immediately make them feel like a part of your school. Cover your classroom door with blue paper; then attach a welcoming cutout. Prepare fish-shaped nametags and attach them to the door so that they can be removed and worn. Splish, splash!

Donna Battista
Parkview Elementary
Valparaiso, IN

Our New "Kinder-garden"!

Plant this home-school connection in the soil of a brand-new year! Give each child a tagboard flower to take home. Instruct her to glue a photo of herself to the center of the flower and ask her family to work with her to decorate the rest of the flower. Have each child bring her flower back to school. Then glue a stem and leaves to each flower and mount it on a board behind a construction paper picket fence. Look who's in bloom!

Missy DiPonio—Gr. K
Bloomfield Hills, MI

Chicka Chicka Boom Boom Look Who's Here In Our Room!

Let's all gather at the coconut tree! To make this literature-related display, cut out tree leaves and a tree trunk from bulletin board paper. Fringe-cut the leaves; then mount the whole tree on a wall. To make a coconut, give a child a brown construction paper circle along with a slightly smaller white one. Instruct the child to write her name in the center of the white circle and then glue that white circle on the brown one. Next, have the child spread a coat of glue on the white circle, but not over her name. Then have her sprinkle flaked coconut over the glue. When the glue dries, have her shake off the excess coconut. Have her spread glue over the brown part of the coconut and then sprinkle crumbled shredded wheat cereal on it. Arrange all these finished projects around the titled coconut tree. See you there!

Krista Miller and Michelle Rinehard
Lincoln Elementary
Findlay, OH

You'll have a place to show off bushels of learning with this year-round wall display. To begin, use a permanent black marker to draw a large basket on brown bulletin board paper. Then cut it out. Mount the basket on a wall along with the title shown. From month to month, give each child an opportunity to make a different contribution to this display. In September, for example, you might fill the basket with child-painted apples; October, pumpkins; November, leaves; December, gifts; January, snowpeople; February, hearts; March, kites; April, butterflies; May, flowers; and June, suns.

Diane Bonica—Gr. K
Deer Creek Elementary
Tigard, OR

Exploring the A, B, Seas!

Dive into the alphabet with this ocean-themed display! Make an undersea scene on your board with drawn or die-cut items, such fish and shells. Then die-cut each letter of the alphabet. Have youngsters help you attach the letters to the bulletin board in the correct order.

Jennifer Weimann—Gr. K
Wollaston Child Care Center
Quincy, MA

Your little ones will be head over heels for this cartwheeling character! Have youngsters help you create a child figure from bulletin board paper. Add wiggle eyes and curling ribbon hair. Place the character on a wall of your room and mount several photos of recent activities to one side. Have students take turns dictating sentences to serve as captions for the photos. The next week, flip the character upside down and leave more photos in her path. Continue until the character makes her way around your room, leaving a trail of memories!

Ann Rowe—Primary Special Education
Picotte School
Omaha, NE

Get into the swing of things with this beginning-of-the-year bulletin board. On a bright-colored background, attach the title, paper grass, and two trees as shown. Tack a bathtub net (used for toys) between the trees to resemble a hammock. Put a stuffed animal or doll (perhaps your school's mascot) in the hammock. Finish the board with personalized apples created by your new students.

Elysa Fisher and Linda Newman
Washington Hebrew Early Childhood Center
Potomac, MD

Welcome new friends with a display of student self-portraits! To prepare, cut two construction paper circles for each child—a slightly larger one from brightly colored paper and a slightly smaller one from white paper. Arrange the colorful cutouts in a circle on a wall or bulletin board; then add the title shown. When students arrive, have them use crayons in a variety of skin tones to create self-portraits on the white circles. Then mount the faces over the colorful circles. Look at our new circle of friends!

Rena Swyers—PreK and Kindergarten
Placentino Elementary
Holliston, MA

Happy birthday! Use a party-themed border to trim a bright background. Write the birthday song on a piece of chart paper, as shown, and then laminate it. Staple the song to the board along with student photos and balloon cutouts. Write each child's name on a separate sentence strip. On a child's special day, pin his name to the open space in the chart and let the celebration begin.

Beverly Nordin—Gr. K
Sykes Elementary
Jackson, MS

This display grows right along with your youngsters! To prepare, mount construction paper grass and a flower stem on a blue background. Have each child trace her shoe on a sheet of construction paper, cut on the outline, and then write her name across the cutout. Mount each child's shoe on the flower to resemble petals; then write the name of the month on the flower. After a few months, add a taller stem to the display and repeat the previous steps. Repeat this activity again at the end of the year and then compare the sizes of the petals and the flowers. My, how you've grown!

adapted from an idea by
Doris Watson
Westview School of Rhymes
Ozark, AL

WHAT'S THE WEATHER?

Keep track of your daily weather with this wonderful weather worm! Decorate a small paper plate to resemble the head of a caterpillar and then mount it on a wall in your room. Each day have a child record the date and the weather on a paper plate or on a small construction paper circle; then add the segment to the caterpillar. At the end of each month, remove the segments from the wall and use them to graph the weather.

adapted from an idea by Shannon M. Lennard—Gr. K
The Dearborn Academy
Dearborn, MI

A PICTURE-PERFECT CLASS!

To create this display, use the pattern on page 23 to make a construction paper camera for each child. Cut each pattern where indicated. Tape a different child's photograph behind each lens opening. Then tape a small piece of foil behind the flash opening. Display the cameras with the title "A Picture-Perfect Class!"

Laura Cozzi—Gr. K
Truman School
Parlin, NJ

Smiles Galore

Here's a back-to-school display that's guaranteed to keep students smiling! Have each child trace a four-inch circle template onto skin-toned paper; then have him cut out the shape and decorate it to create a self-likeness. Mount the completed projects on a large numeral 1 or letter *K*. Display the numeral or letter along with die-cut letters that spell out something like "First grade is '1-derful'!"

Jo Fryer—Gr. 1
Kildeer Countryside School
Long Grove, IL

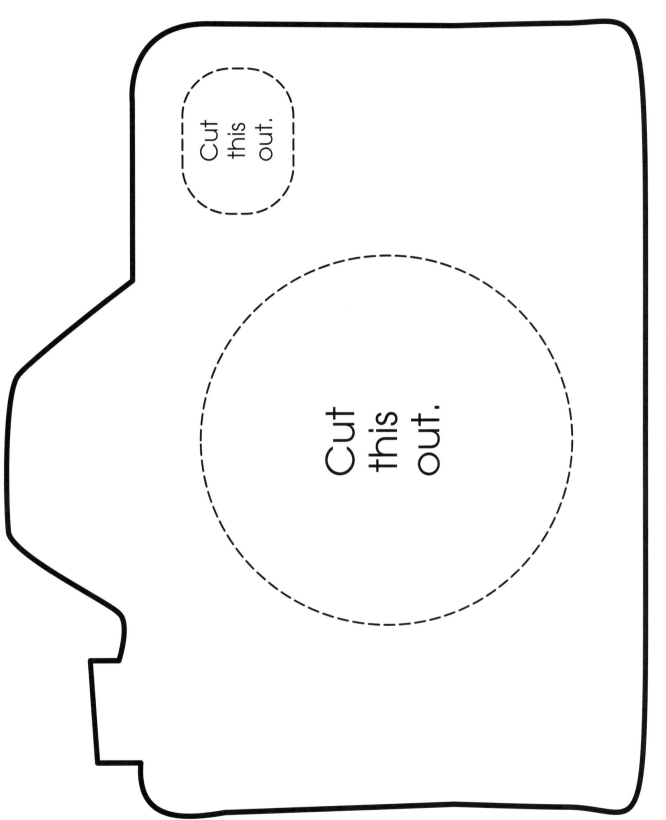

Cut
this
out.

Cut
this
out.

Roll-a-Site

Before school begins, organize your favorite Web addresses on a Rolodex rotary file. List each address and the topic the site covers on an individual card. Also add a short description of what can be found at the site. Then file the card alphabetically by topic in your rotary file. Store the card file and a pen or pencil near your classroom computer. Each time you discover another great Web site, complete a card for it and insert it into your file. The days of staring at a list of bookmarked sites and wondering what information is offered at each one are over! Now you can check your card file and easily put your finger on a Web address for the desired topic.

Jeannie Hinyard
Welder Elementary School
Sinton, TX

honey.com

All you need to know about honey.

recipes, games, books

Perky Plan Book

Brighten your weekly teaching plans by embellishing the pages of your plan book with some well-placed stickers. In addition to seasonal decorations, use stickers to mark the birthdays of your students and coworkers. There's no reason why the time you spend studying your plan book shouldn't be easy on your eyes!

Diane Afferton
Afton School
Yardley, PA

Poetic Organization

Where, oh, where can that poem be? Finding just the right holiday poem or seasonal song is a snap with this organizational tip. In a three-ring binder, place a divider for each month of the school year. Or label file folders in the same manner. Place a copy of each song or poem in the appropriate file. When you need a song to capture the spirit of the season, simply pull one out of the file!

Ericka Lynn Way—Gr. K
Leslie Fox Keyser Elementary
Front Royal, VA

Get Organized

Organize the super activities and reproducibles from *The Mailbox®* with this simple idea! Purchase several three-ring binders and a box of page protectors. Label each binder for a month or season. Then slip your loose teaching materials into page protectors and organize them by topic in the binders. You'll know where to find things, and you'll be keeping your copies in great shape!

Brenda Lorentzson—Gr. K
W.E. Cherry Elementary
Orange Park, FL

Literature Folders

Keep literature-related activities at your fingertips with this organizational system. Label a file folder for each story you plan to use with your students. When you read an idea that relates to one of the stories, file a copy of it in the appropriate folder. You'll soon have several ideas per title. Writing lesson plans will be a snap, and you'll have a handy resource for substitute teachers.

Margarett Mendenhall—Gr. 1
Mary Feeser Elementary School
Elkhart, IN

Catch of the Day!

Fishing for a way to organize counters, markers, pens, and other supplies you use with the overhead projector? Try a tackle box! Purchase a tackle box with movable sections that can be customized to hold your items. Keep the box on the overhead projector cart and you'll never have to cast around for supplies again!

Todd Helms
Pinehurst Elementary
Pinehurst, NC

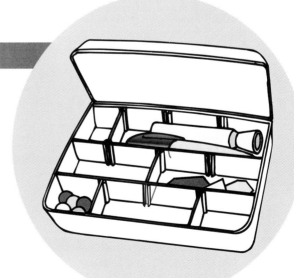

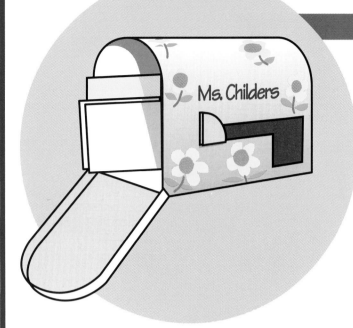

Mailbox Messages

Looking for a way to keep your desk clear of incoming notes, permission slips, and other various messages? Purchase a plastic mailbox at your local hardware store. If desired, use a variety of art supplies to label and decorate it. Place the mailbox near your door. Once parents, students, and faculty members know where to put your "mail," keeping a neat desk will be such a simple task!

Amy Childers—Gr. K
Statesville Christian School
Statesville, NC

Timesaving Storage Tip

Save precious time throughout the year by organizing your teaching charts before school begins. Clip each chart to a hanger and then suspend the hanger from an inexpensive garment rack (available at discount stores). Organize the charts by subject, season, or kind. Store the rack in a desired classroom location. Each time you need a teaching chart, you'll know right where to look!

Janet S. Witmer
Harrisburg, PA

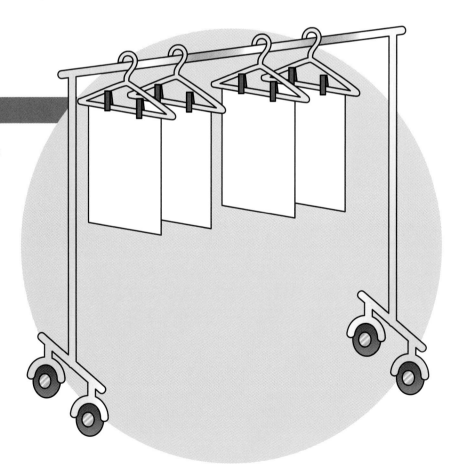

Sticker Rings

Save time and minimize clutter by organizing your sticker collection on metal rings. Hole-punch the top of each sticker sheet as you sort the sheets by theme, holiday, or other desired criteria. Then bind each group of stickers onto a separate ring. Your days of sifting through miscellaneous stickers are over!

Heather Volkman—Grs. 1–2
Messiah Lutheran School
St. Louis, MO

S.O.S. (Save Our Stickers)

Do you find yourself searching through drawers for just the right stickers at just the right time? You'll be stuck on this sticker-storage idea! Label the slots in a small accordion file with themes, seasons, etc. Then neatly file your stickers in the appropriate compartments. When you need a certain type of sticker, you'll know just where to look!

Rhonda Foster—Gr. K

Storage by the Month

Here's another tip that saves you oodles of time during the school year! Label a large stackable container for each month of the school year. In each container store bulletin board cutouts, learning center games, and other items that cannot be filed in a monthly file folder. When it's time to prepare for a new month, grab your monthly file and box and you're ready to get buzzing!

Penny Webster—Special Education
Crossroads Elementary School
Whitwell, TN

FEBRUARY
JANUARY
DECEMBER
NOVEMBER
OCTOBER
SEPTEMBER
AUGUST

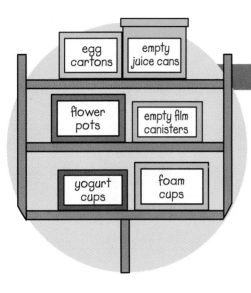

egg cartons

empty juice cans

flower pots

empty film canisters

yogurt cups

foam cups

Schoolwide Storage

Here's a space-saving tip for organizing and storing large quantities of donated items, such as egg cartons, juice cans, and film canisters. Request that shelving be put in an out-of-sight location that is easily accessible to teachers. On the shelves, place empty boxes, each clearly labeled with an item frequently needed for student projects. Then sort donations into the boxes. Solicit parent support to keep the storage area stocked and organized.

Janette Quarles—Speech Therapist Grs. K–2
Glenpool Public Schools
Glenpool, OK

Recycled Storage Containers

Keep these storage options in mind as you set up your classroom.

- **Lids from aerosol cans:** Small and portable, these recycled containers work well inside a desk drawer or at a learning center. They are perfect for storing paper clips, brad fasteners, pushpins, and more!

Lisa Strieker
St. Paul Elementary
Highland, IL

- **Empty film canisters:** These lidded containers are perfect for storing craft beads, wiggle eyes, sequins, and other small art supplies. Use a permanent marker to write on each lid the contents of the container. Or give each child a personalized container in which to store lunch money or tickets.

Cindy Butler
Grapevine Elementary
Vista, CA

Bag of Borders

Organizing bulletin board borders in a shoe storage bag with clear pockets is a smart idea! Suspend the bag inside a closet door. Roll up your borders and store them in the clear pockets. Now you can find the border you need at a glance!

Debra Culpepper
Cedar Road Elementary
Chesapeake, VA

A Bounty of Borders?

Do you need a convenient way to protect and store a bounty of bulletin board borders? Collect a clean, empty plastic frosting container for each border you wish to store. Cut off a sample of the border; then attach it to the front of a container with clear Con-Tact covering. Next, roll up the border and slip it inside the container. Snap on the lid and you're all set!

Mary C. Audsley—Gr. K
Attica Elementary
Attica, NY

Bulletin Board Binder

No doubt you'll make a beeline for this binder of bulletin board ideas time and time again! Label a divider page for each month of the school year and then organize the divider pages in a three-ring binder. Behind each divider page store any bulletin board ideas you have for that month. As you collect new ideas during the year, add them to the binder. If desired, also add photographs of your own classroom displays. You'll have an invaluable resource right at your fingertips!

Susan L. Nowlin
R. C. Waters Elementary
Oak Harbor, OH

Vinyl Tablecloths

Vinyl tablecloths aren't just for kitchens anymore! When you see vinyl tablecloths on sale, stock up on them. They can be used for bulletin board backgrounds, door covers, reading picnics, and counting and graphing lessons. Checkered tablecloths can also be cut to make checkerboards. Save two colors of milk jug lids and you've got the playing pieces too.

DeAnna Martin—Gr. K
Hargett Elementary
Irvine, KY

Quick and Easy Flannelboards

These flannelboards are perfect for little hands or for use in a teacher's lap. Ask your local fabric store for discarded cardboard fabric bolts. Cover the cardboard with felt; then hot-glue it in place. Now let's have some flannelboard fun!

Lori Hamernik—Gr. K
Prairie Farm Elementary
Prairie Farm, WI

Fabric Backdrops

Give your bulletin boards a face-lift with fabric! In addition to being visually appealing, the colorful cloth backdrops are durable and easy to store. To keep costs to a minimum, shop fabric sales and purchase holiday prints out of season.

Stephanie Rising
New Castle, IN

Pocket That Idea!

Need an easy way to organize art projects, games, songs, and other activities that go along with your favorite books? Inside the back cover of each book, attach a library pocket. Then, on a 3" x 5" index card, write the activities that go along with that particular book. Add more cards to each pocket as necessary. No more searching for those wonderful literature extensions!

Debra Nerko—Gr. K
Parkway Elementary School
East Meadow, NY

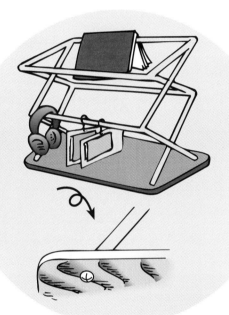

Rackin' Up Big Books

Looking for inexpensive, child-accessible storage for your big books? If you have a little-used laundry drying rack at home or see one at a yard sale, there's your answer! If desired, spray-paint the rack; then screw the legs onto a sheet of plywood. Hang your big books—front covers facing out—on the upper rungs of the rack. Hang earphones, bags of little books, and audio cassettes on the lower rungs. Big-book storage doesn't get any easier than this!

Catherine Turpin—Gr. K
Mohave Valley Elementary School
Bullhead City, AZ

Hook a Book

Taking a few minutes now to organize your book and tape sets will prepare you for fall, plus it encourages this year's students to revisit your collection. Place each book and its corresponding tape in a resealable plastic bag and then clip a clothespin hanger to the bag. Display a sheet of pegboard near your listening center. Insert inexpensive hooks into the pegboard and suspend each bag from a hook. Your students will be all ears!

Alisa T. Daniel—Gr. 1
Ben Hill Primary
Fitzgerald, GA

"Bin" There, Read That!

Reading will be on the rise with this system for easy student selection and shelving. Program each of several large plastic bins with a different symbol; then fill it with books labeled to match. During reading time, set out several bins and assign a group of students to each one. Invite each child to choose books from her bin to read. When reading time is over, have her return her books to the bin with the matching symbol. Rotate bins and books frequently to provide each child with new reading choices. "Bin" there yet?

Kathleen Miller—Gr. K
Our Lady of Mt. Carmel School
Tenafly, NJ

Check Out These Books!

With just a little advance preparation on your part, classroom book checkout can run like a charm! Glue a library pocket inside the back cover of each take-home book. Label a different tagboard card with each book title; then slide each card in the corresponding book's pocket. Next, photocopy a picture of each child in your class. Glue each child's picture to a different library pocket; then personalize the pocket. Arrange all these pockets on a planning chart near the take-home books. When a student is ready to check out a book, she removes the card from the inside back cover and then slides it into her chart pocket. With a simple glance at the chart, each child knows her own book status—and so do you!

Nancy Hopson—Gr. K
Hampton Elementary
Hampton, TN

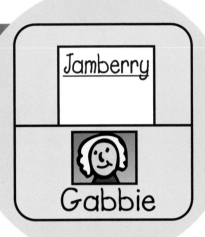

Sentence Strip Storage

Sentence strips are so useful and so handy—but so awkward to store! Well, straighten things out with a long-stemmed flower box. Many florists will donate one for classroom use. It's a perfect fit and can hold quite a lot!

Diane Parette—Gr. K
Durham Elementary
Durham, NY

Slipcover Storage

Looking for a convenient place for youngsters to store their supplies? How about on the backs of their chairs? Purchase some sturdy twill fabric with a colorful design; then sew a simple slipcover to place over the back of each child's chair. Sew a pocket onto each slipcover, inserting a length of elastic in the top hem. The pocket will securely hold a box of school supplies, and it will help keep tables clear and cubbies uncluttered!

Janice Harford—Gr. K
Kelowna, British Columbia, Canada

Crowded Cubby Relief

Create cubby space and save valuable learning time with this clever idea! Use paper grocery bags to create seat packs for students to store their supplies. To make a pack, fold over the top of a grocery bag as shown; then slip the fold over the back of a child's chair. With their supplies at their seats, students will spend less time gathering items and will have more time for learning. The seat packs make great mailboxes and can also be used in a center to hold materials. Replace torn seat packs on your next visit to the grocery store. Paper or plastic? Paper, please!

Elizabeth P. Ridgley and Matthew Periera—Gr. K teacher and student
Haverhill Baptist Day School, Haverhill, FL

A "Shoe-In" for Storage

If your students' cubbies are crammed full of backpacks and lunchboxes, try this idea for keeping papers and artwork neat and organized during the day. Purchase an over-the-door plastic shoe organizer. Hang it over the door or on a wall. Attach a personalized die-cut to each clear pocket; then slip papers into each child's pocket throughout the day. Have youngsters empty the papers into their backpacks before heading home.

Jill Davis—Gr. K
Kendall-Whittier Elementary
Tulsa, OK

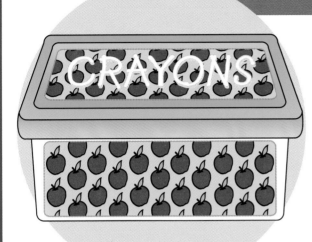

Community Crayon Containers

These durable and eye-catching containers are the perfect place to store community crayons!

Materials for one container:

clean, empty baby wipe container   fabric paint
scrap fabric   iron
fusible webbing   scissors
craft glue

Directions:

1. Iron the fusible webbing to the back of the fabric, following the directions provided with the webbing.
2. When the fabric cools, trim it into desired shapes.
3. Glue the fabric shapes onto the container. Allow the glue to dry.
4. Use the fabric paint to label the container "CRAYONS."
5. When the paint dries, store crayons inside the decorated container.

Kimberly Faraci—Gr. 1, Roberto Clemente School
Brooklyn, NY

Hold It!

Keep all those little classroom items from ending up on the floor—use coffee filters! They're great for holding snacks, math manipulatives, and small art supplies. Invite students who finish early to color, cut, or paint their filters. You'll find endless uses for these convenient and inexpensive holders!

Kathy Shaw—Gr. K   Janet Moody—Gr. K
Roanoke, VA   J. W. Faulk Elementary School
     Lafayette, LA

Fast Photos

Want to make quick sets of photos for class projects? Just grab your school's digital camera (or a Polaroid camera). Take a photo of each child, print it, and then make several photocopies. Store the originals to make more copies whenever you need them. It's a snap!

Pencil Pockets

These kid-appealing pencil holders are a teacher's dream come true! Collect pairs of outgrown or worn-out denim jeans. Cut out the back pockets along with the fabric to which the pockets are attached. Use a hot glue gun, Velcro fastener, or double-sided tape to secure a pocket to each child's desktop. (If your pocket supply is limited, attach pockets to learning center tables, reading tables, and so on.) There you have it—pencil holders that are durable, quiet, and impossible to lose!

Jeanne Brown
Rochester Hills Christian School
Rochester Hills, MI

Desktop Sticker Collections

Between the folds of these nifty desktags, students find the perfect place to store treasured stickers! Label and then laminate a desktag for each child. Fold the desktags in half and secure the bottom half of each one to the appropriate student's desk. Inside, attach some Velcro fastener so the tag will lie flat. Sh! There's a sticker collection inside!

Isabel Pardo—Gr. 1
Bowman Foster Ashe School
Miami, FL

Feed the Pig

This little pig is perfect for motivating your little ones to pitch in and clean up! To make one, use a utility knife to cut an opening opposite the handle of a clean bleach bottle to represent the pig's mouth as shown. Use masking tape to cover the edges of the opening. Next, paint the bottle pink. When the paint is dry, add eyes, felt ears, a pipe cleaner tail, and spools for feet. During cleanup time, you will hear lots of delightful squeals as one student carries the pig around so that others can pick up bits of scrap to feed the hungry paper-eater!

Karen Saner—Grs. K–1
Burns Elementary
Burns, KS

Look Who Popped In!

Taking attendance has new appeal with this "pop-ular" display. To begin, mount the title and a large bowl cutout on a board. Have each child cut out a large piece of construction paper popcorn; then write his name on it. Use pushpins to attach each popcorn piece to the board. As each child arrives, have him pin his popcorn piece above the bowl. With just a glance, you'll be able to tell who hasn't popped in for the day. (If desired, provide some microwave popcorn and invite each child to have a few pieces after he records his attendance. For a fun surprise, set out popcorn-flavored specialty jelly beans one day and just sit back and watch the reactions and comments as children check in for the day!)

Lisa Cohen—Gr. K
Laurel Plains Elementary
New City, NY

From Home to School

Take attendance each day with this easy display! To prepare, cut out a large house and a large school building from poster board. Color the cutouts and add details as desired. Display the cutouts on a wall or bulletin board within children's reach. Next, write each child's name on a separate strip of tagboard. Add self-adhesive Velcro fasteners to the backs of all the name strips and to the house and school shapes. Place all the name strips on the house shape. As each child arrives, ask him to move his name from the house to the school. Then, as he leaves each day, have him move his name back to the house shape. Students will be learning to recognize their names, and you can see at a glance who's at school!

Johnna Lewis—Preschool/Kindergarten
St. Agnes Central School
Mingo Junction, OH

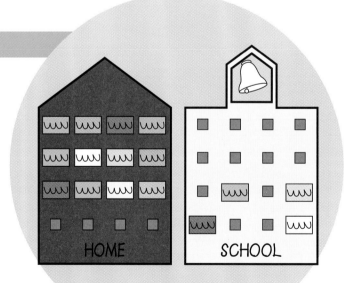

August 29

Adam

Becca

B. J.

Carlos

Frankie

hannah

Mary

Nolan

Sign, Please

This attendance book starts a daily routine that allows children to see their progress in writing their names. Ahead of time, use individual photos to make a supply of sign-in sheets similar to the one shown. Each morning, date one of the sheets and place it by the door. Have each youngster find her photo and sign her name beside it. Store the completed sheets in a notebook. During conference time, the notebook is a handy way to show a part of each student's development. She's on the "write" track!

Mary Beth Heath—Gr. K
Murrells Inlet, SC

No Monkey Business

This attendance system will have your students practicing responsibility while reducing the amount of monkeying around during early morning exercises. To prepare, glue a class set of library pockets to a sheet of poster board. Label each pocket with a different child's name. Then make a class set of construction paper monkeys. Laminate and cut out the monkeys. Post the pocket chart and monkeys within students' reach. Instruct each youngster to place a monkey in her pocket each morning. At a glance, you'll know who is present!

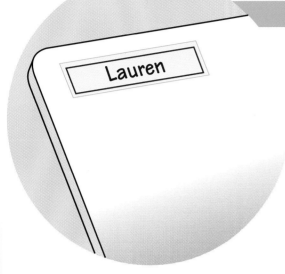

Stick It to 'Em

Have you gotten all those desktops labeled with children's names and incentive charts? Save time by using Con-Tact covering! When adhering name plates, number lines, or other paper-based objects to students' desks, Con-Tact covering not only tapes them down but also covers and protects the surfaces so that there is no need to laminate!

Allissa M. Pendleton—Gr. K
Stanford Elementary School
Stanford, KY

Double Desktags

Two desktags are better than one, and here's why! Sometimes it's difficult to clearly view a desktop tag from a distance. So place a second tag on the side or front of a desk to help classroom visitors read student names more easily. Also, if the second desktag is backed with magnetic tape and you have a magnetic chalkboard, students can use these tags for class graphs, class lists, and so on. Better get a second set of desktags made on the double!

Candi Barwinski
Fleetwood Elementary School
Fleetwood, PA

Portable Desktags

Changing your classroom seating is a breeze when you use these portable desktags! Ask a local paint store to donate a class supply of paint stirring sticks. Spray-paint the sticks; then use a permanent marker to label each one with a different child's name. Next, attach the hook side of a piece of self-adhesive Velcro fastener to each end of the stick. Attach the corresponding loop side to a student's desk or table. Then stick the desktag in place! These portable tags can easily be moved as you regroup students for various activities.

To reinforce the children's first and last names, paint the two halves of the sticks two different colors.

Rachel LeMarbe—Gr. K
Beaumont Elementary
Waterford, MI

Handy Pencil Holders

Here's an easy way to avoid interruptions caused by lost pencils. Attach one side of a small Velcro strip to the top end of a child's pencil. Attach the other side of the Velcro strip to his desk nametag. Have the youngster adhere his pencil to his nametag when it's not in use. Now when he needs a pencil, he'll know exactly where to look!

Kelly Cox—Special Education, Rosedale Elementary
Middletown, OH

News for Nametag Necklaces

Keep nametag necklaces nice and neat with Velcro fasteners. Yes, Velcro fasteners! Attach the hook side of a long strip of self-adhesive Velcro fastener within children's reach on a wall. To store yarn or shoestring necklaces, students stick them to the Velcro strip. That's it!

Stayce Rich
West Side Kindergarten
Magnolia, AR

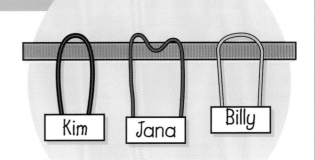

Picture-Perfect

Labeling classroom learning centers is easy with the help of inexpensive, clear acrylic picture frames. Write the title and directions for each learning activity on an index card; then slip each card into a different frame. Place the frames at the corresponding learning centers. When it's time to change an activity, simply slide the card out of the frame and replace it with a new set of directions. Your centers will be neat and organized, and students will easily see the directions for each activity.

Liz Kramer
Boyden School
Walpole, MA

Attention, Please

Help remind your new students of the circle-time scenario with this call-and-response chant.

Teacher: One, two!
Students: Eyes on you!
Teacher: Three, four!
Students: Sit on the floor!
Teacher: Five, six, seven, eight!
Students: Cross our legs and don't be late!

Kari Twedt—Gr. K
Stratton Meadows Elementary School
Colorado Springs, CO

Transitions by the Number

Looking for a simple way to prepare students for a new task? Use the provided poem to prompt youngsters to clear their work areas and give you their attention. They'll be ready in no time at all. You can count on it!

Jennifer Reno—Gr. 1
Adolph Link Elementary
Elk Grove Village, IL

•1•2•3•4•5•

Give Me Five!

I'm on one.
The counting has begun!
I'm on two.
Where are you?
I'm on three.
Where should you be?
I'm on four—
Only one more!
FIVE!

•1•2•3•4•5•

Cleanup Captains

Do you spend more time than you'd like transitioning from center time to the next activity? Here's a tip to ease your load and put the children in charge! After signaling students to begin cleaning up, select a hardworking child from each center to be the captain. Have her inspect the center and dismiss her group to the next activity when she thinks the center is neat and tidy. Remind students that if the captain excuses a group with a messy center, the captain must finish the work herself. Aye, aye, captain—these centers are shipshape!

Ginni Turoff—Gr. K
China Grove Elementary
Kannapolis, NC

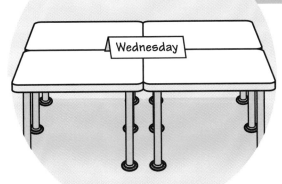

Daily Lineup

Keep students lining up in an orderly fashion day after day! Arrange the students' desks in five groups and name each group for a different weekday. A group lines up first during its namesake day. The first group is followed in line by the group named for the next weekday, and then the next, and so on until all groups are in line. With this systematic approach, lining up quickly and quietly soon becomes a habit!

Pat Hart
C. A. Henning School
Troy, IL

Lineup-Up Chant

This little chant works wonders to help your children concentrate on forming and staying in a line. After practicing the art of lining up, introduce this chant to help with the task at hand.

Our line needs a leader
And it needs a caboose.
We'll make our line straight.
And we'll keep our line loose.

No pushing, no shoving,
Our hands at our sides
As we walk, walk, walk
In our line.

Sandra Steele—Gr. K
Jefferson School
Princeton, IL

Picking Partners

Partner cards are perfect for pairing students. To make a set, divide a class supply of blank cards into two equal stacks. Program each card in one stack with a seasonal sticker so that no two cards are the same. Program the second stack of cards to match the first stack. (If you have an uneven number of students, program one "Wild" card.) When it's time for students to pair up, distribute the cards and ask each youngster to quietly find his match. A student with a wild card joins the pair of his choice. Collect and reuse the cards again and again. Easy *and* fun!

Melanie Cleveland
Blackduck Elementary
Blackduck, MN

Money Manager

Are you looking for individual containers for children's lunch or milk money? M&M's Minis candy containers work great! Remove the label from each tube; then use a permanent marker to write a different child's name on each tube. These containers will accommodate coins up to a quarter's size and rolled dollar bills. As far as emptying the candy from the tubes in the first place? No problem there!

Brenda Harris—Gr. K
Montana Vista Primary
El Paso, TX

Lunch Ticket Butterflies

Make a class supply of these fancy fliers and you'll have fewer lost or misplaced lunch tickets! To make the lunch ticket holder shown, pinch together opposite edges of a four-inch circle of scrap fabric, clip a wooden clothespin around the gathered material, and attach a strip of magnetic tape to the back of the project. Attach a lunch ticket butterfly to each student desk. Or personalize one for each child and then display the bunch on another magnetic surface. On the first day of school, explain the purpose of the butterflies and make sure each child understands that he must personalize each lunch ticket he clips in his holder. One thing is certain—you'll have fewer students fluttering around looking for lost lunch tickets!

Susan Ream
Artman Elementary
Hermitage, PA

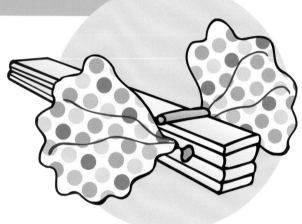

Student Work Folders

Setting aside time before school starts to make a class set of work folders is a wise investment. You'll profit each time a child removes an unfinished paper from his folder and completes it without a reminder from you! Personalize and decorate a colorful file folder for each child. Laminate the folders for durability. If desired, staple or securely tape the sides of each folder to form a pocket. Present the folders on the first day of school. Explain that only unfinished school work goes inside the folders. Also clarify that a student must have an empty work folder before he engages in free-time activities. If work remains in the folder at the end of the day, it becomes homework. Students know from the start that finishing their work is top priority!

Ann McGregor, Emily Carr Public School
London, Ontario, Canada

Follow-up Folder

Providing individualized instruction just got *easier!* Keep a file folder labeled "Follow-up Needed" on your desk. When a child's completed work indicates that he needs additional help with a skill, file his paper in the folder. Each time you have a few free minutes, select a paper from the folder and meet with the corresponding youngster. Spare minutes quickly become teachable moments!

Gina Marinelli
Bernice Young Elementary
Burlington, NJ

Scheduling Tip

Get a clear picture of when individual students attend special classes with this tip. Clip a sheet of clear plastic over each page of your current week's plans and then use a colorful wipe-off pen to program the plastic with desired information. (See the illustration.) Each week transfer the plastic sheet to your current plans and update as needed. A quick glance reveals who is exiting when, as well as when the entire group will be together. A substitute teacher is sure to appreciate this helpful approach.

Darcy Keough—Gr. 1
Doolittle School
Cheshire, CT

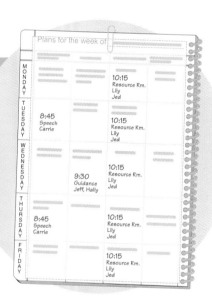

Doable Documentation

Take a practical approach to documenting student behavior. Write each child's name on a Post-it brand index flag. Attach each flag to a different page of a spiral notebook, leaving four blank pages between flags. Program each flagged page with family and medical information about the named student. Label each set of blank pages for the four quarters of the school year. To document student behavior, simply turn to the appropriate notebook page and then date and note your observation. Now that's doable!

Irene Thayer—Gr. 1
Odebolt-Arthur Community School
Odebolt, IA

Picture-Perfect Portfolios

Make this year's portfolios extra special! Photograph each child (using a digital camera, if one is available at your school). Mount each child's photo in the center of a sheet of white construction paper and then ask her to decorate the resulting frame. Slide the child's project inside a large clear plastic envelope and secure it with tape. (Another less expensive option is to use a top-loading multipage capacity sheet protector. Both are available at office supply stores.) There you have it—a picture-perfect portfolio!

Shannon Williams
Woodville Intermediate School
Woodville, TX

Homework Strategy

Start the school year with this proven homework strategy and you'll have fewer homework-related worries. Program the first several pages of a spiral notebook like the page shown. Keep the resulting homework notebook at your desk. When a student does not complete a homework assignment, she writes her name, a description of the assignment, and the due date on the first available line in the homework notebook. She completes her entry when she finishes the homework. In addition to providing you with a handwritten record of homework habits, this book helps students understand that completing homework is their responsibility.

Susan Hearon
All Saints' Episcopal Day School
Florence, SC

Name	Assignment	Due date	Date turned in
Kayla P.	Manners Booklet	Aug. 29	Aug. 30
Hope M.	Manners Booklet	Aug. 29	

October 12
The leaves are...

"Write" From the Beginning!

Here's a simple way to track students' writing progress! Beginning with the first week of school, provide a weekly writing prompt. Have each youngster write and date a response in a journal designated for this purpose. Periodically meet with students to review their entries and discuss their progress. What a pride-boosting form of assessment!

Luella Brunnemer—Gr. 1
Eagle Creek Elementary
Indianapolis, IN

Our Mission Statement

Class spirit and pride abound when youngsters help author a mission statement for your classroom! To begin, lead youngsters in a discussion about why they come to school and what they hope to learn. Write their responses on the board. Next, condense that list into a sentence or two that everyone agrees upon. Write this newly created mission statement on chart paper. Then invite each child to sign the statement. Mount the signed statement on a sturdy, colorful background and post it in a prominent place in your classroom. Periodically read the statement aloud, encouraging children to join in the reading as they are able. Later, choose a different child each day to read or recite the statement during your morning group time.

Genie Merrer—Gr. K
Oldsmar, FL

Positive Puzzles

Reinforce positive behavior with this management idea. To prepare, cut the top of an unused pizza box into large jigsaw puzzle pieces. Explain to your class that positive behavior will earn them one puzzle piece; then mount each earned piece on a bulletin board. When the puzzle is complete, reward your little ones with a class pizza party. For a variation, laminate and then puzzle-cut the top or front of a clean ice-cream carton, popcorn box, or Popsicle box. When the puzzle is complete, reward students with the tasty treats from the box.

adapted from an idea by
Tracey Quezada—Gr. K
Presentation of Mary Academy
Hudson, NH

Caught Being Good!

This catchy chant promotes community within the classroom and helps refocus the class for the next task at hand. To establish a beat and ready the students, alternate between clapping your hands and patting your thighs. Students join in and then begin the chant on your cue, pausing to hear which student you call upon and sitting quietly while he responds. Students enjoy sharing the good deeds of their classmates and occasionally catch a teacher being good, too!

Hey, class! What do you say?
Who have you caught being good today?

Hey, [student's name]. What do you say?
Who have you caught being good today?

Laura Dickerson—Gr. 1
Seawell Elementary School
Chapel Hill, NC

Rules That Make Sense

Rather than present a set of class rules that may not make sense to students, gather students for a game of What Would You Do? To play, pose questions related to student behavior and classroom procedures, such as "What would you do if you had a question for the teacher?" and "What would you do if the fire alarm sounded?" Discuss all responses with the class and then guide students to identify the behavior or procedure that you feel is most appropriate for your classroom setting. List the resulting rules on a chart for future reference. Now that's a question-and-answer game that really teaches!

Darcy Gruber
Delawan, WI

Hands Are for Helping

Are you often reminding your students to keep their hands and feet to themselves? Put a positive spin on that message by saying, "Hands are for helping!" When a child touches something or someone she shouldn't, ask, "What are hands for?" Have the student answer, "Hands are for helping." You'll soon see students reminding one another of this concept when peer conflicts arise. If desired, make a sign like the one shown and post it in your classroom as a handy reminder.

Jean Ricotta—Lead Teacher
Signal Hill Elementary
Dix Hills, NY

Hands
Are for
Helping!

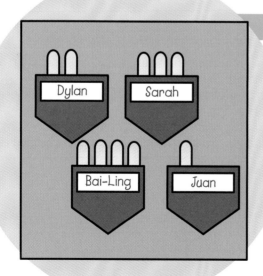

Dylan · Sarah · Bai-Ling · Juan

Positive Pockets

Keep your students on their best behavior by having them collect a pocketful of craft sticks. To store the craft sticks, cut the pockets from several pairs of old jeans. Hot-glue the pockets—one per child—onto a large piece of denim fabric. Tape a name card to the front of each pocket; then hang the piece of fabric on a wall within students' reach. Once a student has accumulated five sticks for good behavior, present her with a prize, such as a trip to a treasure box full of inexpensive goodies. Yippee! It's time to cash in!

Erica Cerwin—Gr. K
Thornton Elementary
San Antonio, TX

Sunshine Basket

Show students that their good behavior brightens your day! Place a small basket within easy student reach. Each time you observe a student displaying exemplary behavior, ask her to personalize a small sun cutout and then drop it in the basket. At the end of each week, draw several names from the basket and reward each of these students with a small treat or happy note. Then empty the basket, and you're ready to reinforce positive behavior the following week. Let the sun shine in!

Gina Marinelli
Bernice Young Elementary
Burlington, NJ

Class Password

Attentive listening and eager cooperation are just two benefits of this top secret behavior plan! Declare a familiar word pairing, such as *bread* and *butter* or *spaghetti* and *meatballs,* as the class passwords. When you say the first word in the pairing, students immediately stop what they're doing, look at you, and say the second word. You can then communicate your message with your youngsters' full attention.

Virginia Toomey—Gr. 1
St. Rene Goupil School
Chicago, IL

A Great Lunch Bunch!

Harvest a bunch of positive lunchroom behavior with this incentive plan! Display a paper grape stem with the title "What a Great Bunch!" Each time the class receives a good report from lunchroom monitors, add a paper grape to the display. When a predetermined number of grapes is earned, reward your bunch with a raisin treat!

Lisa Olson—Gr. 1
Maplewood Elementary
Coral Springs, FL

Here's an easy emergency lesson plan you can leave for your substitute in case you are absent unexpectedly. Leave a copy of *Miss Nelson Is Missing!* by Harry Allard to be read aloud. Then have your substitute help your students write a group story about you, substituting your name for Miss Nelson's. Students will enjoy imagining your adventures while you're out of school, and you'll enjoy reading the story when you return!

Rexanne L. Wright—Gr. K
Independence Elementary
Manassas Park, VA

Substitute Helpers

Here's a creative solution to absent classroom helpers. Substitute helpers! Assign one child to be a substitute helper for the week. Then have that child fill in for any absent helpers. What a super idea!

Barbara Cohen—Gr. K
Horace Mann School
Cherry Hill, NJ

Classroom Jobs

Line Leader	Lauren
Door Holder	Barry
Recess Helper	Karen
Fish Feeder	Felix
Substitute	Alfie

Flag 'em In

Here's a high-flying alternative to blowing a whistle at the end of recess: Wave a special class flag! As each student notices the flag, she tells another child until all are lined up and ready to go. Add motivation to this process by allowing the first child to arrive to hold the flag. For more flag-watching incentive, have students help create the class flag by using fabric paint to make their hand-prints on a sheet of fabric. Sew a pocket narrow enough to securely hold a dowel in place; then slip the cloth over the dowel. Betsy Ross would be impressed!

Cheryl Kiser—Gr. K
Jackson Elementary
Boise, ID

Early Pickup

Reinforce time-telling skills with early-pickup reminders! Keep handy a supply of forms like the one shown. When a parent notifies you that he's picking up his child early from school, program a form with a time that's a few minutes earlier than the planned pickup time; then tape the note to the child's desk. When the parent arrives, the child is ready to go!

Anne E. South
East Oro Public School
Orillia, Ontario, Canada

Dismissal Made Easy

Simplify dismissal during the first week of school with this organizational tip. In advance, prepare different sets of nametags to identify car riders, bus riders, walkers, and children attending afterschool care. Estimate the number of children you will have in each category; then prepare that many blank nametags. As each new student arrives, have her attending adult write the child's name on the corresponding tag. Direct parents to return the tags to school with their children for the first week of school. A few minutes before dismissal, place each child's nametag around her neck; then group students by modes of transportation. Then, when the final bell rings, you can easily see how each of your little ones will get home.

Pam Shaffer—Gr. K
College Park Elementary
LaPorte, TX

A Royal Welcome

Castles and kings and dragons with wings—the goings-on associated with royalty have appealed to boys and girls throughout the ages. So use the regal ideas in this unit to welcome your new court of kids to a kingdom full of learning and fun!

ideas by Joseph Dawes Appleton and Jan Trautman

Classroom Castle

This comely castle will decorate your room in majestic style as well as draw in some of your more reluctant newcomers. To make the castle, cut off three intact panels from a large appliance box. Then cut out a crenellated castle piece from poster board. Tape the crenellated piece to the middle box panel (as shown) using strong tape. Then use a craft knife to cut a door in the middle panel. Paint the castle as desired; then use a permanent marker to add details on the dry paint. Further embellish the castle by gluing on construction paper windows and other details. Top off your castle creation with colorful construction paper or fabric flags that have been taped to plastic straws. To use your castle, choose from the ideas below.

- Use the castle to designate the borders of a center area.
- Have children decorate the inside of the castle as an art option (see "Deck the Halls!" on page 53).
- Use the castle for a backdrop to photograph children individually.
- Post the letter you are studying on the castle door.
- As you study shapes, add shaped construction paper windows or decorations to the castle.
- Change your castle flags to reflect the color you are studying.

Hear Ye! Hear Ye!

Jackson is cordially invited to join Our Royal Classroom!

Please come ready to tell us
- your favorite colors
- your favorite animal
- your favorite foods
- who is in your family

I can't wait to see you on August 15th at 8:00!

Sincerely,
Ms. Leggett

Come, One! Come, All!

To help your new students transition smoothly into the new school year, let them know that you're looking forward to their arrival and you're anxious to get to know them. In advance, make a class supply of the invitation on page 55. Personalize each invitation; then sign it. A few days before school starts, mail an invitation to each child. This special invitation from you will help begin a home-school connection and will also do wonders for making each child feel like royalty!

Royal Door Decor

New students will know just where they belong when they see this royal door decor. To begin, cut out a butcher paper castle tower that will fit on your classroom door. Add colorful construction paper flags and a large paper window. Next, enlarge and trace the friendly dragon (page 56) on sturdy paper. Color and cut out the dragon; then mount it in the castle window. To complete the display, mount any desired room information on the lower part of the castle. Ah, this is right where I belong!

The Crowning Touch

This activity gets your new students involved as soon as they walk in the door. And its crowning benefits include name recognition, fine-motor skills, creativity, and nametags—just to name a few! In advance, make a class supply of the crown pattern (page 55) on construction paper. Cut out the patterns; then write a different child's name on each crown. Arrange the crowns on worktables along with a variety of art supplies, such as crayons, stickers, sequins, jewels, and craft glue. Also have a class supply of sentence strips (to make headbands) and a stapler on hand. As each child arrives on the first day of school, encourage her to find her name and then use the art supplies to decorate her crown. When each child's crown is finished and dry, staple it to a headband. Encourage each child to wear her crown to serve as a nametag throughout the day.

Look Who's in the Castle Today

Each child on your royal roster can participate in making this thematic attendance chart. Then, when your youngsters get in the routine of using it, attendance-taking for you will require only a quick glance at the castle! To make the chart, glue a crenellated, titled cutout to the top of a sheet of poster board. Then tape on toothpick flagpoles and colorful construction paper flags. For each child, glue a labeled library pocket on the poster board. Next, duplicate an attendance card (page 57) for each child and write his name on the emblem. Then invite each child to color his card to resemble himself. If desired, back the cards with poster board for durability; then laminate them. Display all these cards near your attendance chart. To take attendance, instruct each child to find his card and slide it into his pocket on the chart.

Mr. Joe's Class

Look Who's Here!

Tyler | Mary | Austin | Breanna
Ben | Taylor | Kyle
Jack | Allie | Katie

Cody

Maggie

51

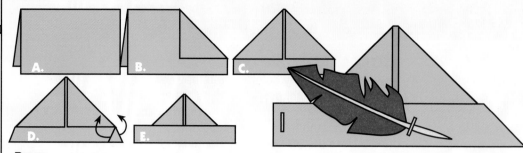

Royal Trappings

Lure youngsters to stretch their imaginations to majestic, faraway places by stocking your dramatic-play area with all the royal trappings. Young ladies-in-waiting will enjoy wearing their royal hats (see illustration), while your boys try out their Robin Hood–style versions. Remnants of richly colored or brocaded fabric can instantly be donned as royal robes. Collect a supply of crown jewels by asking for donations of old costume jewelry. In addition, many stores have Halloween supplies for sale early in the traditional school year. These can be great sources for dress-up supplies.

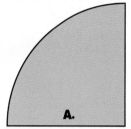
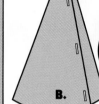

Boys:

To make this hat, fold a 16" x 20" sheet of construction paper as shown in Steps A through E. Then fold under the corners of the brim on one end and staple them to make a pointed brim. Staple the sides together on the other end. Embellish this hat with a real craft feather or a feather cut from construction paper.

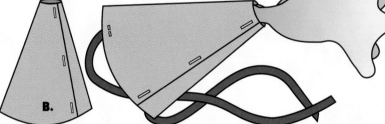

Girls:

For a girl's hat, begin by cutting a quarter-circle from a 16-inch square of construction paper as indicated in Step A. Then roll the paper to form a cone that will fit the child's head (Step B). Before stapling the cone, tape a filmy scarf to the inside of the pointed end and allow it to trail out. (If scarves are not available, substitute crepe-paper streamers.) Next, staple pieces of ribbon to opposite sides of the wide end of the cone to allow the child to tie the hat on.

Sand Castle Kingdom

All you do is provide a few simple supplies, and youngsters will transform your sand table into a fantastic royal kingdom. If you don't already have sand castle molds, take advantage of those end-of-the-summer bargains and purchase a few at your local discount store. Place these molds in your sand table along with a bucket of water, a plant sprayer, plastic shovels, seashells, and other decorative objects such as Unifix cubes or small blocks. Invite children to visit the sand table and use the supplies to explore mixing sand with water to create their own sand castle kingdoms.

Brick by Brick

What better place for building castles than in the block center? Merge your block area with your royal theme by displaying castle pictures nearby. (These pictures can often be found in books or magazines or could be donated by local travel agents.) Also supply other castle-related toys, such as kings, queens, knights, and horses. Encourage your youngsters to examine the pictures for inspiration and then get building!

To promote castle-building enthusiasm, have your camera ready to photograph each completed project along with its builders. Display these photos near the block area. When you have a few pictures collected, surprise children by posting an award ribbon next to each photo. Sometimes children will even invent their own award categories, such as "Tallest Castle Without Falling" or "The Castle With the Most Windows." You never know what those castle-building kids will come up with!

Tallest Castle

Tallest Castle

Deck the Halls!

If you made a classroom castle (see page 50), enlist the help of your little interior decorators to design the royal decor. Position the castle in your art center near a variety of supplies, such as fabric and wallpaper scraps, crayons, paper, craft sticks, craft glue, and a brush for the glue. Encourage each child who visits this center to creatively use the supplies to decorate the inside of the castle. Perhaps one child will draw and frame a portrait of a queen while another child hangs the royal wallpaper. Little hands will get lots of fine-motor practice while creatively working with colors, shapes, sizes, and textures to deck these royal halls.

Graphing Towers

Use these tall towers to make a graphing poster that you can use throughout your castle theme—or even longer. To make the poster, use the tower patterns on page 57. For each tower, photocopy one tower top and as many tower bottoms as you need to have an appropriate number of squares for your class. Mount the towers on a sheet of poster board, leaving a little space at the bottom of each tower. Color the towers; then laminate the poster. Whenever you'd like to do a graphing activity, write a corresponding title on the poster; then paper-clip a label to the bottom of each tower to indicate the categories that you are graphing. Have each student indicate his response by using a dry-erase marker to write his first initial in a space on the appropriate tower. After discussing the graphing results, simply wipe off the laminated surface and you're ready for your next graphing activity.

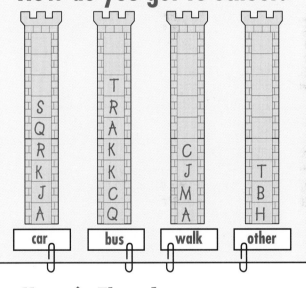

How do you get to school?

car	bus	walk	other
S Q R K J A	T R A K K C Q	C J M A	T B H

Hang in There!

Promote positive self-esteem and get to know your new students as they make these coats of arms. In advance, cut out a large, simple construction paper shield for each child. Use a marker to divide each shield as shown. Working with small groups of children, have each child write her name at the top of the shield. Then prompt the child to design her coat of arms according to the directions below. (If you sent home the invitation in "Come, One! Come, All!" on page 50, your students will have been thinking about this information already.) When all of the projects are done, invite each child to share her coat of arms with the class. Then mount these informative displays on a bulletin board or along a classroom wall.

Section One: Color in this section using your favorite colors.

Section Two: Draw your family.

Section Three: Draw (or cut out and glue pictures of) your favorite foods.

Section Four: Draw (or cut out and glue a picture of) your favorite animal.

53

The Age of Chivalry

"Yes, sir." "Yes, ma'am." "Please." "Thank you." Sounds from the chivalrous past? They don't have to be! Use your castle theme to promote good manners in your classroom. Make a castle tower by taping a crenellated construction paper strip around a clear, plastic cylindrical container. Use permanent markers to draw on bricks, windows, and perhaps a few vines. Then collect a supply of counters, such as marbles or jelly beans.

After an introductory conversation about manners, encourage children to use good manners. Each time you catch a child using good manners, drop one of the counters in the tower. When the tower is full, reward your chivalrous class with a special treat. After your youngsters experience initial success with this reward system, vary it by adding counters for other events, such as an entire circle time or lunch period with good manners. And if, by chance, someone should happen to compliment your class on using good manners, that ought to be worth a handful!

Wasn't That a Dainty Dish...

These colorful castles make a perfect thematic snack during your first days of school.

You will need
- several boxes of flavored gelatin (the number based on your class size)
- hot water (according to the package directions)
- enough clean sand castle molds to hold the prepared gelatin
- one bowl for each castle mold
- lettuce
- speckled jelly beans
- whipped topping

Divide students so that you have one group for each castle mold. Help each group prepare a box of gelatin; then pour it into a castle mold and chill it. (If your molds do not stand independently, nestle them in a container full of rice, beans, or packing pieces.) Unmold the chilled castles onto beds of lettuce to resemble grass. Then scatter speckled jelly beans on the lettuce to resemble rocks. When you're ready for a snack, have each child scoop a serving of castle into a bowl and top it with a dollop of whipped topping.

Pam Crane

Once Upon a Time

Here's a selection of kingdom-related literature that you can use as read-alouds or to stock your reading center.

Kate's Castle
By Julie Lawson

King Bidgood's in the Bathtub
By Audrey Wood

The Paper Bag Princess
By Robert Munsch

The Princess and the Pea
Retold by Harriet Ziefert

Hear Ye! Hear Ye!

_____ is cordially

invited to join

Our Royal Classroom!

Please come ready to tell us
- your favorite colors
- your favorite animal
- your favorite foods
- who is in your family

Sincerely,

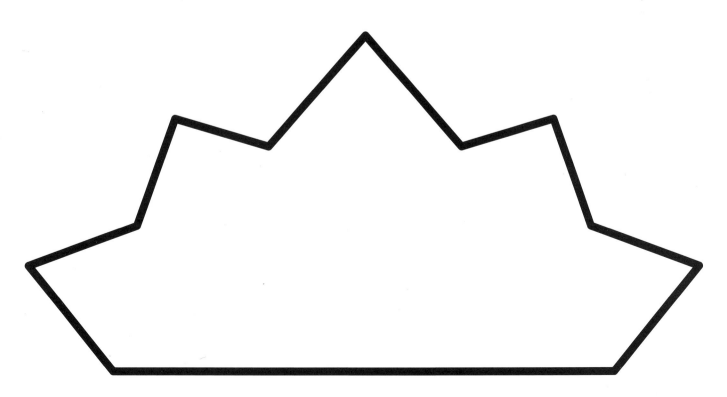

Dragon Pattern
Use with "Royal Door Decor" on page 51.

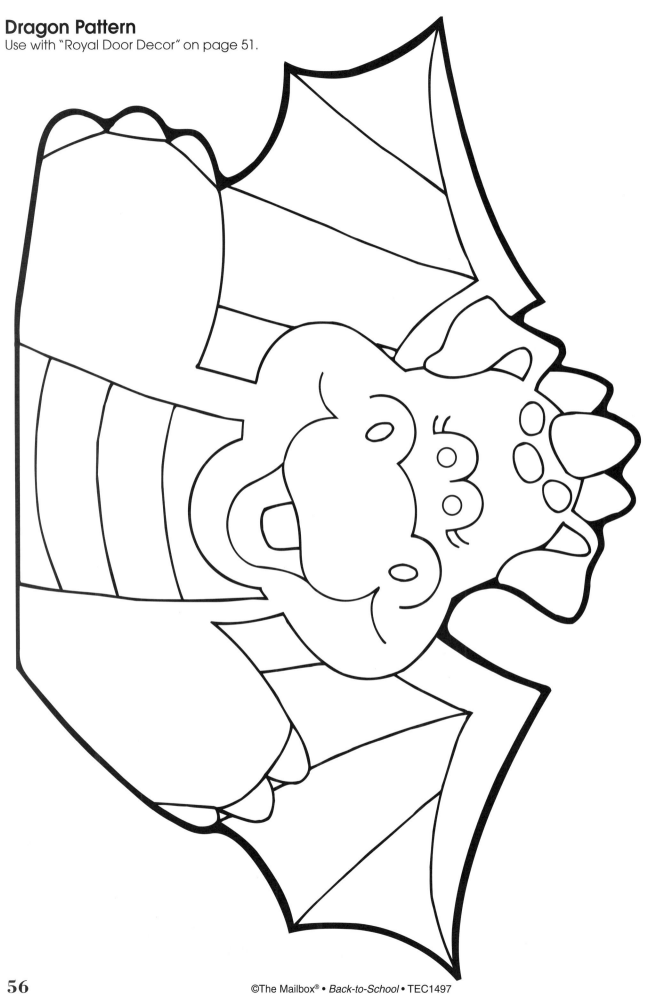

Tower Patterns

Use with "Graphing Towers" on page 53.

tower top

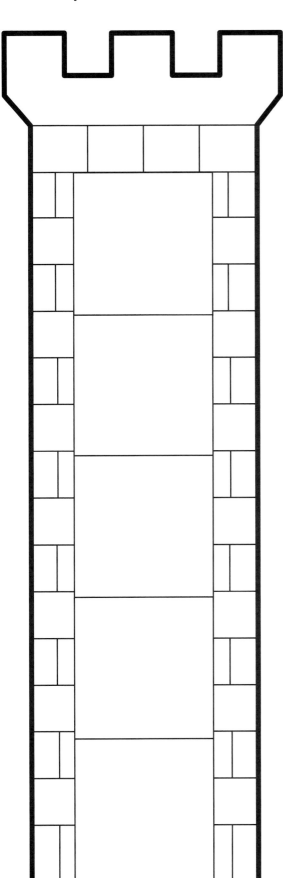

tower bottom

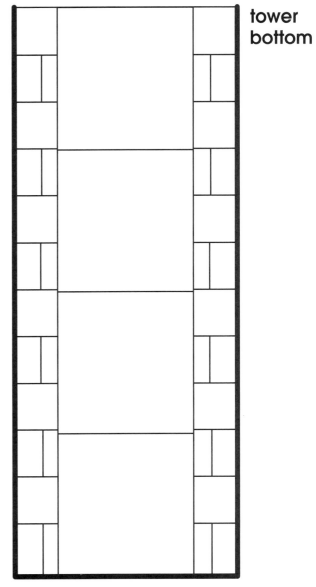

Attendance Card Pattern

Use with "Look Who's in the Castle Today" on page 51.

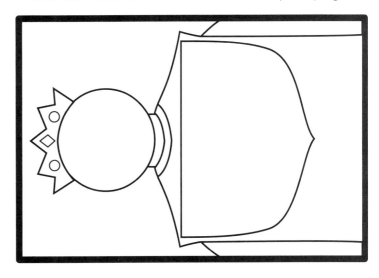

HANGING OUT IN SCHOOL

Aah! Nothing says comfort like the feel of a favorite T-shirt! Bring this same comfort into your classroom during the first days of school with these T-shirt theme ideas that are one-size-fits-all!

ideas by Lucia Kemp Henry

Welcome!

Show your new students that you are eager to meet them with these special T-shirt greetings. Make a class supply of page 62 on colored construction paper. Personalize each T-shirt, sign your name, and then cut it out. If desired, cut a small slit at the top of the T-shirt's pocket and insert a treat—such as a new pencil, a lollipop, or a stick of gum—as shown. Then tape the treat to the back of the cutout to hold it in place. This timely note from you is sure to make each child feel like he'll fit right in!

This Must Be the Place

Your new students will know right where to go when they see this lineup of colorful T-shirts outside your door. To make the display, cut out two narrow lengths of bulletin board paper and tape them to your wall to resemble clothesline poles. Next, attach the ends of a length of thick yarn to the poles to serve as the clothesline. Cut out eight large T-shirt shapes from different colors of construction paper. Use a wide-tip marker to label each of the seven shirts with a different letter from the word "Welcome." Then label the eighth shirt with your name and room number. Mount each shirt to the wall so that it slightly overlaps the clothesline. Finish the display by clipping colorful clothespins to the shoulders of each shirt as shown. Glad you're here!

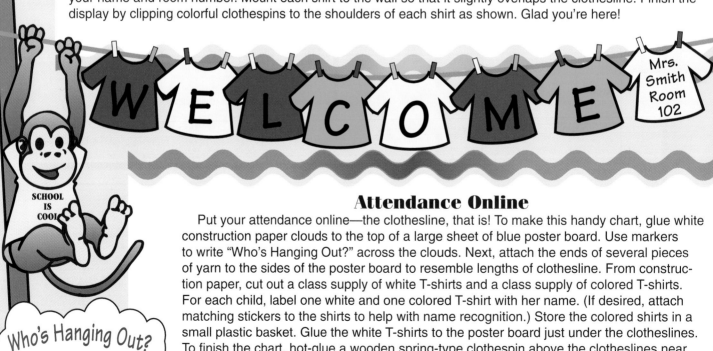

Attendance Online

Put your attendance online—the clothesline, that is! To make this handy chart, glue white construction paper clouds to the top of a large sheet of blue poster board. Use markers to write "Who's Hanging Out?" across the clouds. Next, attach the ends of several pieces of yarn to the sides of the poster board to resemble lengths of clothesline. From construction paper, cut out a class supply of white T-shirts and a class supply of colored T-shirts. For each child, label one white and one colored T-shirt with her name. (If desired, attach matching stickers to the shirts to help with name recognition.) Store the colored shirts in a small plastic basket. Glue the white T-shirts to the poster board just under the clotheslines. To finish the chart, hot-glue a wooden spring-type clothespin above the clotheslines near the top of each white T-shirt as shown. Then mount the chart to a bulletin board or wall within youngsters' reach.

As you welcome each child on the first few days of school, help her find her colored T-shirt and encourage her to pin it to her space on the chart. As your youngsters become accustomed to using this chart every day, taking attendance will be a breeze!

Special Tees

Celebrate a birthday, a lost tooth, a student of the week, or some other favorite happening by making a whimsical T-shirt for the honoree to wear during the school day. Use fabric paints and any other embellishments of your choice to decorate a shirt for the designated occasion. (You may want to have two or three birthday shirts on hand, just in case!) Then invite the special student to wear this special tee on his special day. Afterward, simply wash and dry the shirt for the next celebration.

BEAUTIFUL COLORS

They Come in All Colors

What better way to display colors in your classroom than with T-shirts? Cut out a large T-shirt shape from a piece of 12" x 18" colored craft foam in each color you want to represent. Use fabric paint, glitter glue, or a permanent marker to label each T-shirt with its corresponding color word. If desired, tape a small hanger to the back of each shirt. Then display the shirts on a bulletin board or wall along with a title.

"Plen-tee" of Helpers

Continue the T-shirt theme throughout your room with this classroom job display. Photocopy page 62. Mask out the text on the T-shirt; then use the modified copy to duplicate a construction paper T-shirt for each job in your classroom. Label each shirt with a different job title and a corresponding illustration. Then cut out the shirts and laminate them for durability. Use an X-acto knife to cut a small slit at the top of each pocket.

To make name cards, write each child's name (or glue his photo) on a separate 1½" x 2½" piece of card stock. Laminate the cards if desired. Then glue a craft stick to the back of each name card.

To use the helper display, insert a child's name card into the pocket of each T-shirt. Then simply switch the names periodically to give everyone a turn at being a "migh-tee" fine helper!

59

T-Shirt Show-and-Tell

Break the ice with this short-sleeved sharing session. As youngsters bring in their favorite T-shirts (from "Welcome!" on page 58), collect them in a laundry basket. During your first circle time, hold up a shirt and ask its owner to stand or come to the front of the group. Encourage him to say his name, describe his T-shirt, and then explain why it is his favorite. Be sure to include yourself in the sharing too! At the end of the introductions, have each child wear his shirt and sing the movement song below.

A T-Shirt That's Just for You
(sung to the tune of "Daisy, Daisy")

Find a T-shirt, any ol' color will do.
Find a T-shirt. Pick one that's old or new.
Then put on your shirt. You can do it!
There's really nothing to it.
You're off to school.
You look so cool
In a T-shirt that's just for you!

Point finger in different directions as if choosing.
Pretend to hold up a shirt.
Pretend to put on a shirt.
Cheer with arms.
Walk in place.
Smile and strut.
Hold hands out to the side and turn in a
 circle as if modeling.

Meet Our "Facul-tee"

Extend the sharing in "T-Shirt Show-and-Tell" to include members of your school staff as a fun way of introducing them to your youngsters. Arrange for each staff member that your students need to meet—such as the school secretary, librarian, custodian, principal, and music teacher—to bring his favorite T-shirt to school. Then, after the classroom T-shirt sharing, lead youngsters on a school tour to meet and greet other staff members and hear about their favorite tees. Now you've given your little ones something to associate with each new face!

Trendy Tees

Use this idea to practice fine-motor skills and encourage creativity with your little fashion designers. Make several simple T-shirt templates from tagboard (or use the T-shirt pattern on page 62). Have each child choose a color of construction paper; then help her trace and cut out a shirt shape. Use a marker to label each child's shirt with her name. Then provide a variety of decorative materials—such as glitter glue, sequins, buttons, stickers, and fabric scraps—for each child to use to decorate her T-shirt. When the projects are complete, remove the T-shirts that spell "Welcome" on the clothesline created in "This Must Be the Place" (page 58). Then hang the new T-shirt collection on the clothesline. (You might need to add another clothesline to accommodate everyone's shirt.) Finish the display by adding the title "Look Who's Hanging Out in Our Room!" These one-of-a-kind T-shirts are sure to be conversation starters for anyone hangin' around in the hallway.

LOOK WHO'S HANGING OUT IN OUR ROOM!

Katie

Cassie

Noah

Allen

Jamar

Devon

T-Shirt Tales

You'll get to know your new students even better as they work on these individual booklets. And your new students will be getting to know some of their thinking, fine-motor, and artistic skills! To prepare, duplicate pages 63–65 for each of your students. Encourage each child to complete her pages. (See the directions below.) Then help each child cut out her pages, stack them in order, and staple them together along the left side. Invite each child to share her book with the group and then take it home to share with her family. "Tee-rific" bookmaking!

Cover: Write your name in the space provided.
Page 1: Color the shirt your favorite color.
Page 2: Cut out a magazine picture of your favorite food; then glue it to the page.
Page 3: Write your age on the shirt.
Page 4: Color the head to look like yourself. Then write (or dictate) to complete the sentence on the shirt.

61

T-Shirt Pattern

Use with "Welcome!" on page 58, " 'Plen-tee' of Helpers" on page 59, and "Trendy Tees" on page 61.

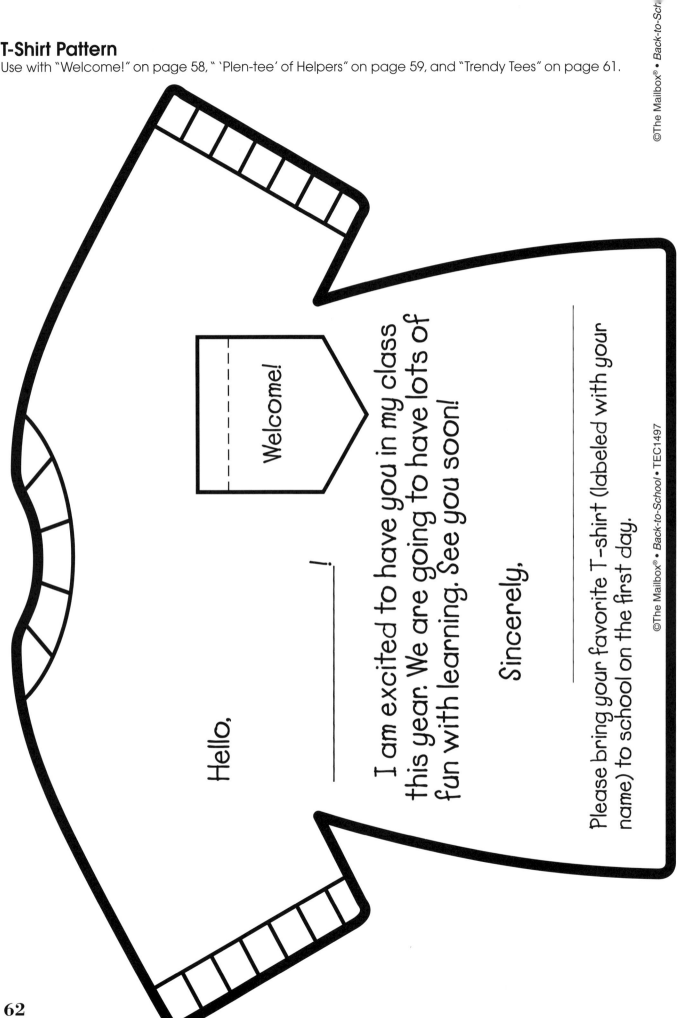

Welcome!

Hello, _____!

I am excited to have you in my class this year. We are going to have lots of fun with learning. See you soon!

Sincerely,

Please bring your favorite T-shirt (labeled with your name) to school on the first day.

©The Mailbox® •Back-to-School• TEC1497

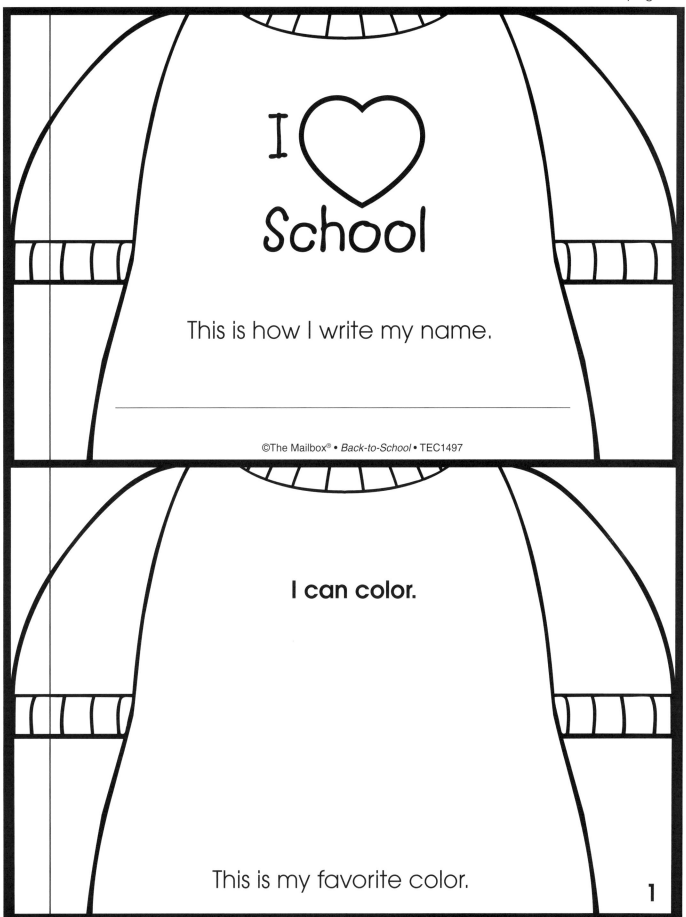

I ♥ School

This is how I write my name.

_____

©The Mailbox® • *Back-to-School* • TEC1497

I can color.

This is my favorite color.

1

Booklet Pages
Use with "T-Shirt Tales" on page 61.

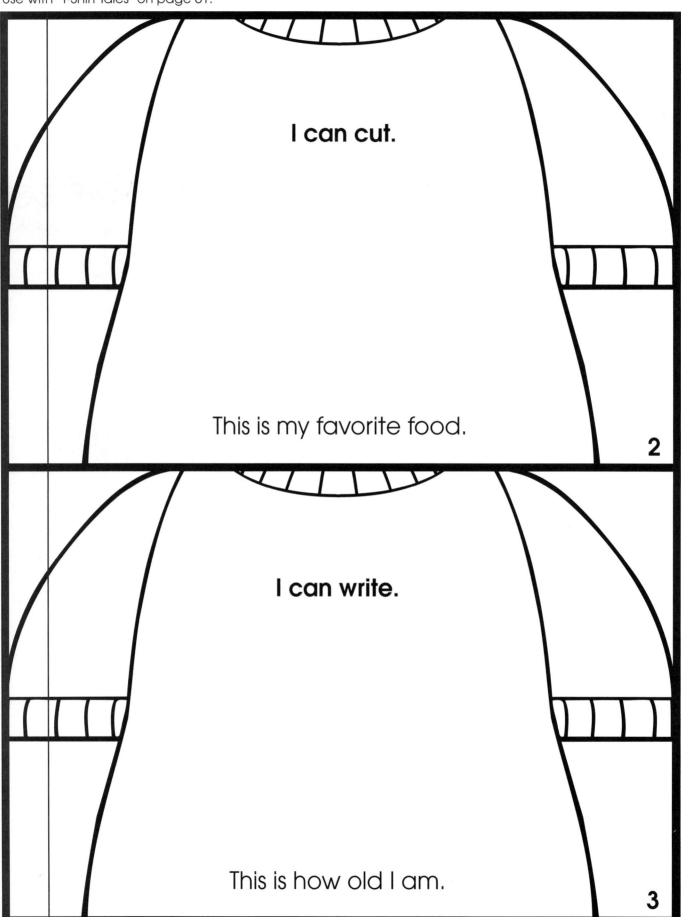

I can cut.

This is my favorite food.

2

I can write.

This is how old I am.

3

I like to

4

Ms. Ridout, our principal

School Safari

This indoor safari will introduce your youngsters to their new surroundings and to the school staff with an added element of fun! In advance, leave a small stuffed jungle animal or picture card in each place you plan to visit with students. Explain to youngsters that they will be going on a safari through the school in hopes of seeing jungle animals along the way. Then don your safari hat, grab your instant camera, and guide youngsters through the school. Introduce students to the people and places that will be significant to them, and have them look for rare jungle animals. At each stop on the safari, take a photo of the exotic animal along with the special person or place. After you return to the classroom, place the photos in an album and invite youngsters to revisit their safari tour.

Monkey See, Monkey Do

This whole-group game will allow your youngsters to show off their silliness as it gets them moving! Have the class stand in a circle. Designate one child to be the lead monkey and to stand in the center of the circle. Instruct the rest of the group to chant, "Monkey see, monkey do. Show us, [Emma], what you can do!" Have the featured child perform an action, and instruct the rest of the class to repeat it. Then have the monkey in the middle choose someone to take her place and continue the game.

Welcome to the Jungle

This catchy song will help your new arrivals get to know one another! Have youngsters hold hands and walk in a circle while singing the song. As the two names are sung in Line 2, have the youngsters named meet in the middle of the circle and shake hands. Repeat the song until each child has been featured.

(sung to the tune of "The More We Get Together")

Welcome to the jungle, the jungle, the jungle.
Welcome to the jungle, [Miranda] and [Mike].
The animals play here, and we'll have a great day here!
So welcome to the jungle! We're glad you are here!

Mary Wore Her Red Dress

Feature each child's name and chosen specialty of the day with this familiar song. First, share the book *Mary Wore Her Red Dress and Henry Wore His Green Sneakers,* adapted and illustrated by Merle Peek. Then have each child stand, in turn, and say her name and what she would like the class to sing about. Then sing away! Extend the use of this song by using it in call-and-response style to encourage children to remember their classmates' names. To do so, sing the song asking a question, such as "Who is wearing stripes today?" or "Who is wearing brown boots?" Encourage the class to respond by singing, for example, "Jess is wearing stripes today, stripes today, stripes today…"

Judy Richmond—Gr. K
Good Shepherd Lutheran
Pekin, IL

All Join Hands!

Here's an activity that will reinforce listening skills and honor diversity as well as similarities among your students. Begin by seating your children in a circle. Call out a direction such as one of those suggested below. When the specified children stand, ask them to move to the middle of the circle and join hands. Then have them sit down where they are. Repeat this process many times, having children move from group to group. Make your last direction one that will include everyone, such as "Stand if you are a student in [Ms. Wiklendt's] class." Have all the children join hands and form a circle like the one they were in at the beginning of the activity. Guide children to summarize that they are all alike and different in many ways, but they are all part of the same class!

Stand and hold hands if
- you are wearing [sneakers]
- you have [blue] eyes
- you like [chocolate] ice cream
- you have a [brother]
- you have a [dog]

Jamie Wiklendt—Gr. K
Chattahoochee Elementary
Duluth, GA

The Davis Tree

Family Trees

Use this "tree-mendously" helpful display when first learning to recognize all your new students' parents and primary caregivers! On the first day of school or during open house, take a photograph of each student with his significant adult(s) and any other family member present. Mount each photograph onto a tree cutout; then label each tree with the family's name. Arrange the trees on a bulletin board titled "Our Family Trees." Your little ones will love looking at the display, and you will have a handy tool to help you quickly identify parents during those hectic first few days!

Sharon Davis—Gr. K
Lafayette Elementary
Oxford, MS

Adam!

Higgety, Biggety Bumblebee

Can you say your name for me? This catchy rhyme draws the attention of your linguistic and auditory youngsters while the movement keeps those kinesthetic kids involved. To begin, seat students in a circle. Say the rhyme below; then toss a soft ball or beanbag to a child. Ask that child to say his name. As abilities permit, encourage the whole class to repeat that name, whisper that name, clap the syllables, and say the beginning sound. Then say the rhyme again, asking the child who is currently holding the ball to toss it to another child when the rhyme has been said. Continue in the same manner until each child's name (and yours) has been said.

Higgety, biggety bumblebee—
Can you say your name for me?

Melissa Jackson—Gr. K
Miano School
Los Banos, CA

Meet the Class

Instead of sending home the interest inventories that your students complete on the first day of school, collect and publish them in a three-ring notebook. For durability, insert the students' papers into plastic page protectors. Also include a photograph of each student with his interest inventory, if desired. Then arrange for each child to take home the notebook so he can introduce his family to his new classmates. Each time a new student joins your class, update the notebook and then invite him to take it home for the evening so he can quickly get to know his new classmates!

Lynn Lupo-Hudgins
Austin Road Elementary
Stockbridge, GA

Me Bags

Build self-esteem and help students get to know each other better with this back-to-school activity! For each student, glue to the front of a paper bag a poem like the one shown. Have each child take his bag home and return it on a designated day with an item inside that represents something special about himself. Ask each child to share his item with the class and answer questions from his classmates.

Catherine Salvini—Multiage Grs. 1–2
Morningside Community School
Pittsfield, MA

Me
Please help me decide
What item goes inside,
Something about me
For all my friends to see,
What I like or do
That makes me special too!

Off the Wall

Incorporating classroom furnishings and supplies into first-day lessons is a fun way to introduce students to their new surroundings. Have students sort attribute blocks by shapes or Unifix cubes by colors. Read aloud a fiction and a nonfiction book from the classroom library, and ask students to use the classroom clock to answer time-related questions. Use a globe or map to review the continents and oceans of the world, and refer to the birthday display to create a class graph of student birthdays. This introduction to the classroom is sure to make students feel right at home!

Pamela Reifsneider—Associate Teacher
Newtown Friends School
Newtown, PA

School Map

This first-day activity familiarizes students with their school, and it shows them that a map represents a real place! Post a simple map of the school on a bulletin board. Ask students to name important places around the school, and list their ideas on the chalkboard. Next, take the class on a walking tour of the school. Be sure to visit each important place and take an instant picture there. When the tour is over, enlist your students' help in mounting the pictures around the edge of the school map and using lengths of yarn to connect the photos to their corresponding map locations.

Jennifer Alexander
Stocks Elementary
Greenville, NC

Making Friends

Foster friendships with this first-day activity. To begin, ask students what they can learn about their teacher by just looking (hair color, height, and so on). Then reveal several things about yourself that cannot be seen, such as a favorite place to visit, favorite hobbies and foods, something that scares you, and so on. Help students understand that to make a friend it is important to learn things that cannot be seen. Then, on provided paper, have each child write his name and illustrate himself doing something he enjoys. Hole-punch the pages and compile them in a binder labeled "Making Friends." Encourage students to look at the volume to find classmates who share their interests. If desired, also keep a supply of hole-punched paper handy so students can add illustrations to the book throughout the year.

Betsy Meyer
Hugh Cassell Elementary
Waynesboro, VA

Blue-Ribbon Buses

Look who's in the driver's seat! For this back-to-school idea, make a class supply of a yellow construction paper bus that has several windows. Instruct each student to glue a small photo of herself in the driver's seat and then provide information about herself in each window. Ask each student to cut out her bus and share her busload of information with the class before you post the projects around the room. Students will be ready to roll into a new school year with these clever introductions to their classmates.

Gina Parisi—Grs. 1–6 Basic Skills
Brookdale School
Bloomfield, NJ

Pal Posters

Promote friendship and build self-esteem with a poster-making activity. To make his poster, a child uses large letters to write his name at the top of a 12" x 18" sheet of white construction paper. Below his name he illustrates his self-likeness. Next, he writes on his poster five activities he enjoys and five words that describe his personality. (Provide assistance as needed.) Set aside time for each child to share his poster with his peers. Then exhibit the projects in a school hallway where other potential pals can take a peek.

adapted from an idea by Kirsten S. Reynolds
South Elementary School
Andover, MA

Meet the Staff

Students will quickly become acquainted with your school staff when you make this class big book. To begin, take a picture of each staff member hard at work; then glue each photograph onto a large, separate sheet of construction paper. Patterned after the text of Eric Carle's *Brown Bear, Brown Bear, What Do You See?* label each page as shown, changing the name to correspond with the person in the photo. Before binding the pages together into a book, display them in a hallway for all to enjoy.

Linda K. Lilienthal—Gr. K
Hayes Center Elementary
Hayes Center, NE

Duck, Duck, Who?

That old favorite game of Duck, Duck, Goose is a great one to use when it comes to learning names! First, play the game in the traditional way. Then add little twists. For example, when It sits down, ask him to say the name of his chaser. At another time, announce that It must say the goose's name as he chooses her. Or even write each child's name on a goose cutout. Place all the cutouts in a box. Then have It secretly choose a goose from the box. Have him whisper the name to you (for confirmation) and then choose that person as the goose during his turn. You'd better run!

Kelly J. Sickle—Gr. K
Oak Grove Primary
Oak Grove, MD

Action-Packed Scavenger Hunt

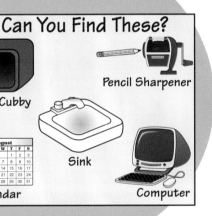

When your new students visit your classroom just before the start of the school year, send them on a scavenger hunt! Make a simple scavenger hunt sheet (similar to the one shown), listing places in the classroom you want students to see. Duplicate the list for each child. Make the hunt more active by posting at each spot a sign that asks youngsters to perform an action. For example, post a sign near the pencil sharpener that says "Can you sharpen your pencil?" Near the soap dispenser at the sink, post a sign that says "Can you make the soap come out?" Little ones will become familiar with their new classroom and gain a sense of accomplishment.

Lisa Wilkinson—Gr. K
Loveville School
Loveville, MD

Mystery Student

Here's a fun way for students—especially shy ones—to get to know each other! Each day secretly select a child to be the next day's mystery student. In private, record the child saying, "Hi! I like to [three favorite activities]. Who am I?" Remind her not to reveal that she's the mystery student! The following morning, play the recording and give the class three chances to guess the child's identity. If the class correctly identifies the student, write her name on the "Solved" side of a chart like the one shown. If the class can't solve the mystery in three guesses, write her name on the "Unsolved" side. Students are sure to become better acquainted!

Carrie Hursh—Gr. 1
Harrison Elementary
Harrison, OH

MYSTERY STUDENT

SOLVED	UNSOLVED
Emily	Kayla
Rhea	Josh
Zach	
Tyrone	
Hannah	

I like to read scary books.

Nancy

Classmate Puzzles

What's in the cards? A get-acquainted learning center! Each student cuts a blank 4" x 6" card jigsaw-style to make a two-piece puzzle. She assembles the puzzle and marks each piece to indicate the top. On one half, she writes her name and illustrates a self-portrait. On the other half, she writes a sentence about herself. Store students' prepared puzzle pieces in a gift bag at a center. A student assembles the puzzles to learn about her classmates!

adapted from an idea by Catherine Broome
Melbourne Beach, FL

A Word-Search Welcome

Here's a first-day activity that's sure to please! Prepare a word-search puzzle and a corresponding word bank that includes each child's name and your name. After students complete the activity, ask each child to introduce himself to the class and then reveal where in the puzzle his name is located. Send the papers home with students at the end of the day so they can share with their families the names of their new classmates and teacher!

Nell Roberts—Gr. 1
The Covenant School
Charlottesville, VA

NCMLXR
DAVIDP
ZIPLAT
KBELRF
LFOYTL

Which do you like better?

Pizza	Ice Cream
😊	😊
😊	😊
😊	

Get Acquainted With Graphs

This daily math activity not only introduces students to graphing, it provides a great conversation starter to discuss likes and dislikes. In advance, mount onto tagboard a photo of each child. Trim as desired; then attach a strip of magnetic tape to the back. Store the pictures in a basket near a magnetic markerboard. Draw a simple bar graph on the board and program it with a yes/no or preference question as shown. Read the question aloud and then invite each child to find her picture and place it on the appropriate side of the graph. Discuss the results with students and introduce concepts such as more, less, and equal. Ask a new question each day to help students get acquainted. I wonder if more youngsters like pizza or ice cream better?

Meet Me!

These special posters will boost self-esteem right off the bat. For each child, fold a 12" x 18" sheet of construction paper in half. Program the right side of the paper with a child's name. Next, cut out a construction paper child shape; then glue it to the left side of the poster. On one of the first days of school, invite each child to color and decorate the cutout to look like himself. Then have him glue on magazine pictures or drawings that tell about himself. Encourage each child to share his completed poster during a group time.

adapted from ideas by Linda Rasmussen—Gr. K
Donner Springs
Sparks, NV
Dorothy Weigandt—Gr. K
Ethan School, Ethan, SD

Predictions, Please

For a fun first-day writing activity, have each child describe what he thinks he'll learn during the school year. Ask him to use his best handwriting for the project and then tuck his prediction in his portfolio. Plan to return these papers to students at the end of the year. Not only will each youngster enjoy reading his first-day prediction, he'll surely see evidence of the progress he's made.

Pam Zettervall
Willard Model Elementary
Norfolk, VA

The Name Game

Syllables are counted and grouping takes place when students participate in this activity. Review with students how to clap the syllables in a word. Then have each child clap the number of syllables in his name. After each child has determined his number of syllables, have students group themselves with others who share the same number. Then count the total for each group and graph the results.

To extend this activity, review the titles of school personnel with students. Then have youngsters clap the syllables of each word as you repeat it slowly. Instruct students to count the number of claps for each word. After they get the hang of it, invite each youngster to call out a word for the group to clap. *Prin-ci-pal* has three syllables!

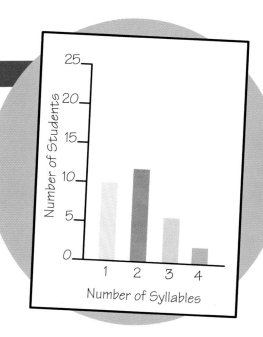

And Cupcakes for All!

How can you make sure every child gets to celebrate her birthday with her classmates? Make a request on your school supplies list. Along with scissors and glue, ask each parent to send in a box of cake mix and a container of frosting. (For those who are unable to contribute, you may need to furnish several boxes or ask a few parents to send in extras.) Then make cupcakes for the class on each student's birthday. Summer birthdays can be celebrated as half-birthdays (a July 10 birthday would be celebrated on January 10) or at the end of the school year. Now that's fair!

Joyce Wilkerson—Grs. PreK–K
Jefferson Elementary
Sherman, TX

Happy Birthday Book

Here's an inexpensive and creative way to celebrate a student's birthday. Have each classmate write a letter to the honored child on decorative paper. Bind the students' letters, a letter from you, and a title page between two poster board covers. For added appeal, wrap each poster board cover in birthday paper and use curling ribbon to bind the project. Then lead the students in singing a familiar birthday tune and present the book of letters to the birthday child. Plan to recognize all your students' birthdays—even those that occur during the summer—with this letter-perfect idea.

Anita De La Torre
Hutton Elementary
Chanute, KS

Handcrafted Birthday Cards

Here's a birthday card project that really takes the cake! Each child folds a 12" x 18" sheet of white construction paper in half and writes on the back of the card "Made just for you by [student's name]." Then she decorates the front of the card, making the most spectacular birthday card she's ever seen. Collect the cards and inside each one write "Happy Birthday From the Whole Gang!" To recognize a child's birthday, select a card she did not make and ask each of her classmates to sign it. Ask the classmate who designed the card to present it to the birthday student. Be sure to establish a plan for celebrating summer birthdays throughout the year!

Suzie Robinson—Gr. 1
Pioneer Elementary School
Neoga, IL

Birthday Books

Use this idea to start collecting a variety of birthday-themed stories. Instead of (or in addition to) having parents provide birthday treats to eat, ask them to treat the class to a new birthday book in honor of the birthday child. Inside the front cover, write the child's name, her birthday, and the current year. Share this special book with your children; then have the birthday child choose another book from the collection for you to read aloud. Be sure to read the inside front cover of this book, too. Happy birthday to you!

Susan Bunyan
Dodge City, KS

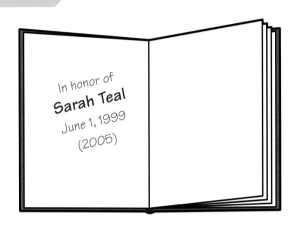

In honor of
Sarah Teal
June 1, 1999
(2005)

Birthday Rap

Have your youngsters get in the rhythm of this birthday rap by starting off with a clap, clap, snap pattern! Instruct students to complete the pattern three or four times before reciting the rap. For each birthday, substitute the child's name in the second line.

We are friends, and we're here to say
It's [Connor's] birthday—hooray, hooray!
[He'll] have cake and ice cream too.
We hope [his] wishes will all come true!

Sharon Manley—Gr. K
Israel Putnam School
Meriden, CT

Birthday Graph

Here's a first-day activity that teaches and pleases students! Display a large bar graph titled "Birthday Graph." With your students' help, list the 12 months of the year on the graph. Next, have each child write her name and birth-date on the graph for the correct month and lightly color the corresponding square. Pose questions about the completed graph for students to answer. Then, after a review of monthly abbreviations, have each child label a 9" x 12" sheet of one-inch graph paper for a birthday graph and then color the spaces to correspond to the posted graph. Students will be proud to share these first-day projects with their families, and you'll feel good about the concepts you've covered!

Pamela Williams
Dixieland Elementary
Lakeland, FL

Jan.						
Feb.						
Mar.						
Apr.						
May						
June						
July						
Aug.						
Sept.						
Oct.						
Nov.						
Dec.						

Customized Business Cards

Melrose Park School
Mrs. Michelle Lechel
Room 10
school: 555-0123
voice mail: 555-0124

Please feel free to call me with any questions or concerns that you may have regarding your child's education.

To make it easy for parents to contact you, use a computer to customize business cards especially for their use. Include your name, the name and phone number of your school, and an email address and/or voice mail number where messages can be left. Print the information on blank business cards purchased from a local office supply store. To create magnetic cards, attach the cards to precut business card magnets (also available from office supply stores). It's an inexpensive way to encourage parents to stay in touch!

Michelle Lechel
Melrose Park School
Melrose Park, IL

Extraordinary Emails

Sending good news to parents just got easier! At the start of the school year, invite parents to share their email addresses with you. Use the addresses throughout the year to send positive notes about student performance and behavior. Imagine a parent's delight when she logs on and finds an email bearing good news about her child!

Shannon T. Jones
John Redd Smith Elementary School
Collinsville, VA

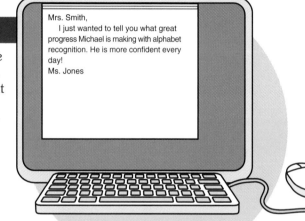

Mrs. Smith,
   I just wanted to tell you what great progress Michael is making with alphabet recognition. He is more confident every day!
Ms. Jones

Timesaving Forms

Count on parents to give this communication convenience rave reviews. Prepare a form for each of several common occasions that require a parent note. Duplicate each form on colored paper to make two copies per child. Staple each student's forms into a booklet. Distribute the booklets at open house or send them home with a note of explanation. A parent removes a form from the booklet as needed, completes it, and returns it to school with her child.

Joan Turner
Oakbrook Elementary
Ladson, SC

Absence

My child, _____ ,was absent
                (student's full name)

on _____ because
        (all dates)

_____ .
    (reason for absence)   (date)

_____
(parent signature)

"Note-able" Communication

Use this bright idea, and you can be sure that your notes to parents won't get lost in the shuffle! Keep a supply of vividly colored envelopes on hand. When you have a message or notice that requires immediate attention, tuck it in an envelope before giving it to the appropriate student to take home. Parents will recognize the colorful correspondence at a glance!

Sandy Preston
Brockway Area Elementary School
Brockway, PA

Mr. and Mrs. Saunders

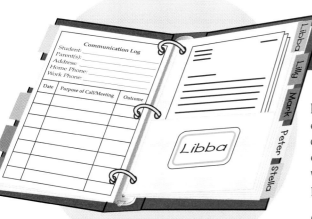

Communication Binder

Keeping track of parent communication just got easier! Prepare a communication form similar to the one shown. For each student, program a copy of the form and label a tabbed divider with pockets. Secure the materials in a binder so that each student's form faces the corresponding divider. Store written correspondence in the pocket and jot down notes from phone calls and meetings on the form.

Christie Peiffer—Gr. 1
Seabourn Elementary
Mesquite, TX

Back-to-School Made Simple

Use this idea to help organize the overwhelming odds and ends that can come with the start of school. For each child, label the outside of a two-pocket folder as shown. Add the child's name, your name, transportation information, and any other relevant information. Then gather your beginning-of-school paperwork, such as your welcome letter, a school handbook, and insurance forms. Indicate which of these papers must be returned to school by stamping them with a recognizable symbol, such as a star. (Be sure to write the code that you choose to use on the inside of the folder.) When you meet each parent, simply hand her a folder and encourage her to take it home and look over the information at her own pace. Then each child can use this folder to transport papers between home and school.

Beth Randall Davis—Gr. K
Lemira Elementary
Sumter, SC

All I Need to Know About Kindergarten

Please return to school. Thank you!

October 26, 2005

Dear Jessica,

I hope you are having a good day at school. I just wanted to tell you how much I love you. And also, I love to hear you sing!

Love,
Dad

P.S. I can't wait for our music night together!

From Parents With Love

Doesn't everyone enjoy receiving a love letter every now and then? Your students will too—especially when the letters come from their own parents! Ask each parent to write a loving letter to his child and then drop it off at your school office or mail it in care of you. When you feel the time is right, don a construction paper postal hat and deliver the letters to the addressees. Encourage children to read their letters aloud (or ask you to do it) if they wish. Then store the letters for later. Whenever a child comes down with the blues—or just because—read his letter again!

Latresa Bray—Gr. K
Townview Elementary
Dayton, OH

Topic Trackers

Turn parents and children into topic trackers by asking them to help locate items for upcoming themes or topics. You can do this in your weekly newsletter: just write in the topic and add a deadline for bringing the items to school. Then make a class supply. Parents and children instantly become involved in your school topics. Now that's the track of purposeful parent involvement!

Judy Clifford—Gr. K
Central Elementary
Point Pleasant, WV

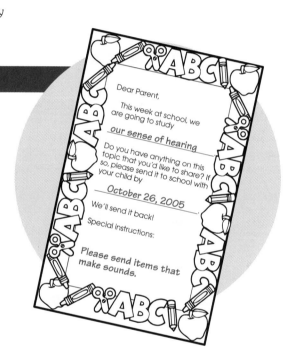

Dear Parent,

This week at school, we are going to study

our sense of hearing

Do you have anything on this topic that you'd like to share? If so, please send it to school with your child by

October 26, 2005

We'll send it back!

Special instructions:

Please send items that make sounds.

Please cut out 32 pumpkins.

Due October 11.

Partnering With Parents

Here's a solution for parents who want to volunteer but are unable to help during school hours. Prepare packets with simple assignments and have parents complete them at home. To make one packet, write the directions and the due date for the assignment on a sheet of paper; then staple the paper to a large manila envelope. Fill the envelope with all the necessary materials to complete the assignment. Send the packet home with the child and have him return it to school when completed.

Ginny Haithcock—Gr. K
George Hall Elementary
Mobile, AL

Notes? No Problem!

Sending personalized notes home to parents is a snap with this idea! For each child's parent, program and sign a supply of decorative note sheets. Then file all the note sheets by name in a file box with *A–Z* dividers. When you observe a student doing something worth sharing, grab one of his personalized note sheets and jot down a quick message. The note is ready to go in just seconds! This system not only saves time, but you can also see which parents have not yet received positive news.

Rhonda Foster—Gr. K
West Central Elementary School
Francesville, IN

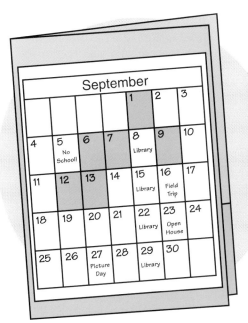

At a Glance

Parents will appreciate this home-school connection, which shows them all they need to know at a glance! To prepare, program the days on a monthly calendar with your class events for the month, such as field trips, snack duty, and special parties. Make a copy of the calendar for each child; then staple the calendar to the cover of a pocket folder. At the end of each day, place the child's work in her folder; then color the appropriate day on the calendar to indicate the child's behavior (for example, green=great, yellow=fair, red=needs improvement). Send home the folder for parents to review and sign; then have the child bring the folder back to school the next day.

Michele Moore—Gr. K
David Crockett Elementary
Marshall, TX

"Deck-orate" the Halls!

When your students partner with their parents, your halls will be decked to the nines—all year round! Near the end of each month, make a class supply of a seasonal shape or an enlarged copy of clip art for each child. Send the shapes or designs home along with a note asking parents to help their children decorate them as desired. They can use stickers, Cheerios cereal pieces, ribbon, glitter glue, nuts and bolts—anything goes! When youngsters return their projects, display these festive, family-made projects along a hallway. Each time parents visit, they'll know they helped make your hall shine throughout every season.

Judy Clifford—Gr. K
Central Elementary
Point Pleasant, WV

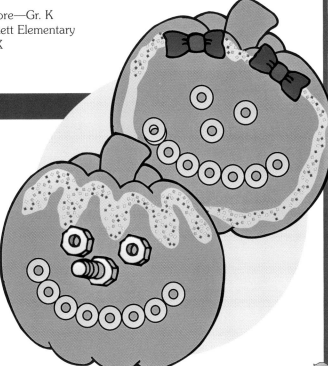

A Patchwork Quilt of Teachers

Patch together this crafty introduction to your teaching staff for everyone to enjoy during open house. Give each teacher, assistant, support staff, or parent volunteer a sheet of white construction paper. Ask her to fill the sheet with pictures (from photos, magazines, catalogs, postcards, or craft books) that reflect her hobbies, interests, experiences, or talents. Mount each finished sheet on a larger sheet of construction paper of a complementary color. (Alternate background colors if desired.) Then staple the finished projects on a bulletin board, adding additional sections with your favorite quotes on education or warm greetings, if needed. Use a marker to add stitches to give it that quilted look. Everyone will enjoy trying to match each teacher to a quilt section.

Taryn Lynn Way—Gr. K
Los Molinos Elementary School
Los Molinos, CA

Coloring Tables

Keep young siblings busy during your open house or parent conferences by setting up one or two coloring tables. Simply cover a table with inexpensive paper and set out a basket of crayons. They'll stay busy, and you can display the family art later for everyone to enjoy!

Anne Rideout—Gr. K
Sandy Elementary
Sandy, UT

Masterful Invitations

Here's just the touch to spark each parent's interest in open house. First, enlarge the invitation on page 83 and duplicate it to make a class supply. Then encourage each child to color a picture about school in the frame. Several days before open house, have each child take his invitation home and present it to his parent. Parents will enthusiastically anticipate open house when they see these invitations embellished with their own children's artistic masterpieces.

Sue De Riso
Barrington, RI

Every day I'm off to school,
And I think that's really cool!
But now it's time for you to see
This very special part of me!

Please come to open house on

Monday, October 3, 2005

Busy! Busy! Busy!

Do you have an open house near the beginning of the year? Try this project to give parents and family members a glimpse into just how busy their little ones are. Start by having each child use art supplies to decorate a paper plate to resemble himself. Tape a large craft stick to the back of each plate. Then tape each craft stick to the back of a chair. Drape each child's paint shirt (or a shirt that he brought in) over his chair so that it appears as if the child is sitting at his desk. On each desk (or table space), display something that a child might do during the day. For example, you might put pattern blocks in one child's space, math counters in another, and color-word cards in another. There's just no end to how busy we can be!

Colleen Thompson
Chosen Valley Elementary
Chatfield, MN

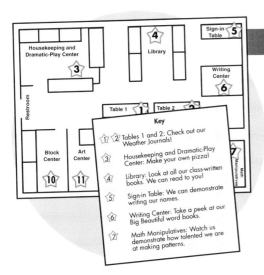

Classroom Walk of Stars

Prepare your little ones to shine during open house with this special guide. In advance, display a numbered star cutout at each point of interest in your classroom. Then draw a simple map of your classroom, using correspondingly numbered stars. Next, write or type a key describing what parents should note at each stop along the way. Then make a supply of the map and key. Before the big night, familiarize your students with the maps so that they'll be able to guide their parents along. As each parent and child arrives for open house, give the parent a map and a key; then encourage the child to guide her parent through all the points of interest on your classroom walk of stars.

Sue Creason—Gr. K
Highland Plaza United Methodist Kindergarten
Hixson, TN

Parent-Made Magnets

Turn the tables at this year's open house by helping parents make special gifts for their kids! Provide small magnets, wooden craft hearts, craft glue, glitter pens, and paint markers at a workstation. After a parent decorates one side of a wooden heart, he glues a magnet on the back. When the project dries, he displays it on one side of his child's desk. Have students use their parent-made magnets to suspend cut-and-paste papers, artwork, or other projects that require drying time.

Carmen Rufa—Gr. 1
Watervliet Elementary School
Watervliet, NY

Pitch In!

You're sure to hit a few home runs with this open house display, which gets parents involved! Cut out a supply of construction paper baseballs. On each baseball, write a needed classroom item, such as tissues or graham crackers. Next, label a construction paper baseball glove as shown; then tape it to the outside of a large, clean, empty coffee can. Put the baseballs in the can and set it near your classroom door. At open house, invite parents to pitch in by taking a baseball from the can and donating the item listed on it. Batter up!

Shelly L. Kidd-Hamlett—Gr. K
Helena Elementary
Timberlake, NC

Fresh Play Dough

Tired of dried-out play dough? Ask parents to make fresh play dough each month! At a parent visitation night near the start of the year, put out a sign-up sheet for any parents who are interested in making play dough for your class. Each month, send home a play dough recipe to one or two families that have signed up, and ask them to send in the play dough within a week. You might ask for specific colors or let the parents surprise you! When the new play dough arrives, divide the old dough and send it home with students. You'll get lots of fresh play dough, and parents will get a fun recipe they can use again at home!

Barbara Cohen—Gr. K
Horace Mann Elementary
Cherry Hill, NJ

No-Cook Dough

Ingredients:
4 c. flour
1 c. salt
1 ³⁄₄ c. warm water tinted with food coloring

Preparation:
Combine the flour and salt in a bowl; then add the warm water. Knead the dough for ten minutes. Keep the dough refrigerated in an airtight container.

Classy Clips

These student-made display clips are perfect for greeting class-room visitors and showcasing students' work. Provide each student with a head and shirt–shaped cutout made from poster board. Have each student create and label a likeness of herself using markers, crayons, construction paper, and glue. Laminate the cutouts for durability and hot-glue two clothespins to the back of each shirt. Hole-punch the top of each project and use monofilament to suspend it from the classroom ceiling. As students complete work they'd like to exhibit, clip it to their cutouts. What a wonderful way to showcase students' work during open house and throughout the year!

Robin Pizzichil
Evergreen Elementary School
Collegeville, PA

Invitation
Use with "Masterful Invitations" on page 80.

Every day I'm off to school,
And I think that's really cool!
But now it's time for you to see
This very special part of me!

Please come to open house on

Handprint Puzzle

Here's a first-day-of-school project that parents will treasure! Visit your local craft store to purchase a class supply of blank jigsaw puzzles. Or simply use 5" x 7" pieces of poster board. Paint a child's hand with tempera paint; then have him press a handprint onto the blank puzzle or poster board. Use a permanent marker to write the child's name near the print, or have him write it himself. Allow the paint to dry. If you're using poster board, puzzle-cut the finished project. Put each child's pieces in a separate zippered plastic bag; then staple the provided poem to the bag. What a great keepsake!

Angie Bonthuis—Gr. K
Gilbert Elementary
Gilbert, IA

Let's keep this puzzle with my handprint.
When we put it together, you'll say,
"Now I remember how big you were,
At school, on the very first day!"

Here are my hands with ten fingers in all—
My first mark in school to hang on the wall.
As years go by, I'll remember and say,
"My hands and I had a very good day!"

Here Are My Hands

Dip your hands into this first-day memento that will mean a lot to both children and parents. To begin, copy the poem shown on white paper; then duplicate it for each child. Next, have each child select a color of paint and make handprints on the top part of a sheet of construction paper. When the paint is dry, glue the poem to the bottom part. Read the poem together, inviting each child to read along. Also encourage each child to count the ten fingers in her handprints and on her own hands. That sounds like a very good day!

Melissa Jackson—Gr. K
Miano School
Los Banos, CA

One-of-a-Kind Border

These student-made borders are perfect for trimming a back-to-school display! Give each youngster one or more strips of connected paper-doll cutouts similar to the one shown. Have him color desired details. Then mount the prepared cutouts on sentence strips. You'll have a unique bulletin board border, and students will be pleased to have helped!

Deborah Ridgeway—Gr. 1
Warford Elementary
Kansas City, MO

"Safe-Tees"

Near the beginning of the school year, have each child bring in a plain white T-shirt. Enlist the help of some parents to help tie-dye the T-shirts using your school colors. Then have youngsters wear the shirts when your class goes on a field trip. Your students will be recognizable as part of your group, but the shirts won't give away any information about their names or school to strangers.

Jean Ricotta—Lead Teacher
Signal Hill Elementary
Dix Hills, NY

Apple Trees—One Foot Tall

These little apple trees make a big impression on all who see them! In advance, prepare a large container of warm, soapy water for easy cleanup. Have each child cut a treetop from green construction paper and then glue it to the top of a light blue sheet of construction paper as shown. Next, have her step in a shallow pan containing a thin layer of brown paint. To create a tree trunk, help each youngster position her foot on her paper and make a print. Then have her clean her foot with soapy water. Next, have her use a red bingo dauber to print apples on her tree. It's harvest time!

Diane Bonica—Gr. K
Deer Creek School
Tigard, OR

Fancy Apples

These apples are unique and that's no yarn! Begin with a tagboard apple cutout. Working atop a paper towel, cover the apple with a thin layer of glue. Next, lay individual four-inch strips of red yarn horizontally across the apple. Keep the yarn lengths close together and let the ends extend beyond the edges of the cutout. Continue until the apple is completely covered with yarn. When the project is dry, trim away excess yarn. Glue a green felt leaf and a brown felt stem to the project and it's ready to adorn a class tree.

Rebecca Racciato—Gr. 1
Five Points Elementary School
Bangor, PA

Welcome Back!

_____'s Journal Prompts

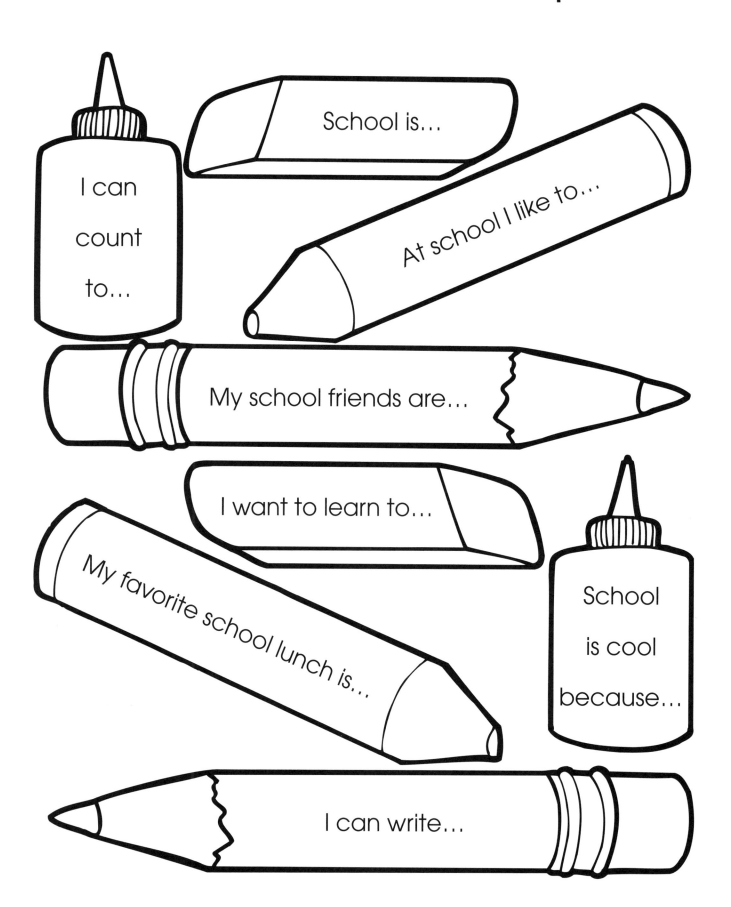

School is...

I can count to...

At school I like to...

My school friends are...

I want to learn to...

My favorite school lunch is...

School is cool because...

I can write...

School Supplies

Look at each row.

What is missing?

 Draw it.

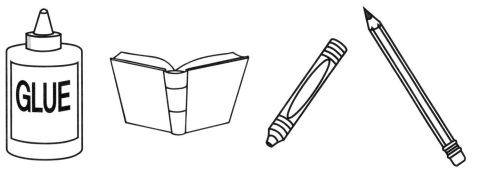

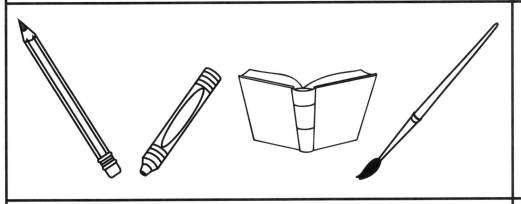

As Easy as 1, 2, 3!

✂ Cut. 🧴 Glue the pictures in order.

1	2	3

✏ Write 1, 2, and 3 in the boxes to show the order.

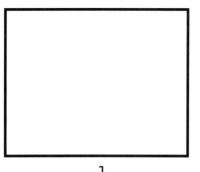
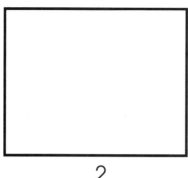
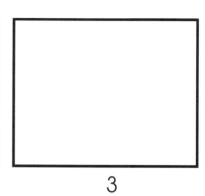

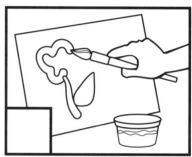

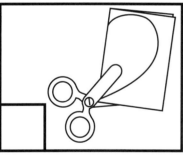
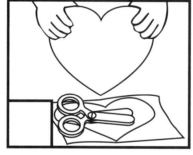

Name _____

School Shirts

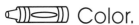 Write.

Color.

Word Bank				
green	blue	black	yellow	white
red	purple	orange	brown	

Readiness Route

Trace the path the bus will travel.
Look at each house.

If you see a letter, color the house.

School Tools

Color the objects with matching letters in each row.

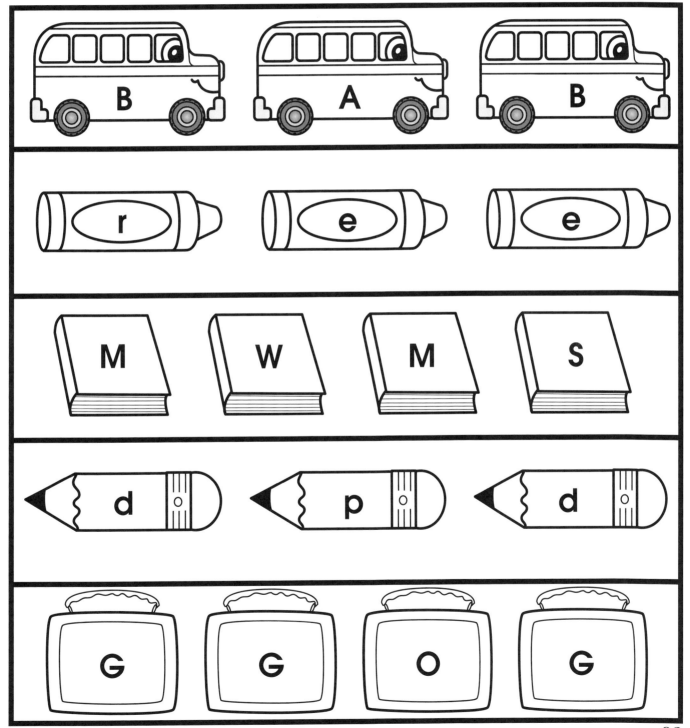

To School We Go

Find the letter pairs.

Color each object in the pair the same color.

Draw a line from each bus to its matching school.

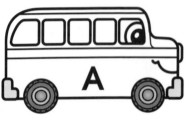

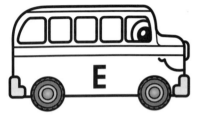

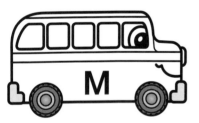

94

Bus Buddies

 Cut. Match the letters. Glue.

95

Everyday Helpers

What does each helper use to do his or her job?
Cut and glue to match.

A **crossing guard** helps us cross the street.

A **mail carrier** delivers the mail.

A **firefighter** puts out fires.

A **doctor** listens to your heart.

A **police officer** protects the town.

A **hairstylist** cuts hair.

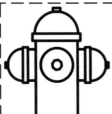